TRIUMPH
B O O K S

TRIUMPHBOOKS**.COM**

THE
GEORGIA BULLDOGS FANS'
BUCKET LIST

THE
GEORGIA BULLDOGS FANS'
BUCKET LIST

JASON BUTT

TRIUMPH
B O O K S

Library of Congress Cataloging-in-Publication Data

Names: Butt, Jason.
Title: The Georgia Bulldogs fans' bucket list / Jason Butt.
Description: Chicago, Illinois : Triumph Books LLC, [2017]
Identifiers: LCCN 2017009807 | ISBN 9781629373324
Subjects: LCSH: Georgia Bulldogs (Football team)—History. | Georgia
    Bulldogs (Football team)—Miscellanea. | University of Georgia—
    Football—History. | University of Georgia—Football—Miscellanea. |
    Football—Georgia—History. | Football—Georgia—Miscellanea.
Classification: LCC GV958.G4 B87 2017 | DDC 796.332/630975818—
    dc23 LC record available at https://lccn.loc.gov/2017009807

This book is available in quantity at special discounts for your group or organization. For further information, contact:

Triumph Books LLC
814 North Franklin Street
Chicago, Illinois 60610
(312) 337-0747
www.triumphbooks.com

Printed in U.S.A.
ISBN: 978-1-62937-332-4
Design by Andy Hansen
Page production by Alex Lubertozzi

This book is dedicated to my parents, Gene and Sally,
for their love and support.

Contents

Foreword

In his book, *The Georgia Bulldogs Fans' Bucket List*, Jason Butt does a tremendous job of portraying what a college town can provide to the overall experience of playing, coaching, or following a team. You will enjoy his unique ability to weave together the UGA history and its rich heritage while also detailing some of the great places to visit.

I have spent 54 of my 72 years on a college campus, starting as a quarterback at North Carolina State in 1963. Being involved in and around the university community has given me and my family more than just an education and a job. I have met many lifelong friends inside and outside of athletics.

There are five-star athletes who I have recruited, coached, and played with and also many who weren't as highly rated but a key part of our teams' successes. Also integral to that success were the many students, professors, and administrators I met through the years who were my friends outside of sports.

Anyone who goes to a school develops a bucket list of what he or she wants to achieve, and I'm sure, as you go through the book, you will enjoy the areas described by Jason. Certainly every place I've been has provided me with many of my favorite places to go. But in particular, Athens and UGA represent 21 years of happiness for me. I love being a part of this college environment. Being named Georgia's head coach was a thrill for me. I have met and developed so many relationships on and off the field here.

I was offered three major jobs—at North Carolina, North Carolina State, and Oklahoma—for big money during my tenure at UGA. Even though we started out with limited scholarships because of probation and were competing with two teams in our division—Florida and Tennessee—that won national championships, I felt that we were laying the foundation.

It was difficult to lose my team with three years left on my contract, but the bottom line was we didn't win quickly enough against the teams we needed to beat. Basically, I had a decision to make about what I wanted to do with my career. We decided not to move away because our plan would have been to get back in coaching in the next year, and that would have involved another move. Staying in Athens left us with our friends and allowed us to continue to enjoy everything we had enjoyed outside of athletics—the fine dining, great weather, and easy access to Atlanta, which allows you travel to anywhere you would want to go. Tennis and golf are two of my favorite activities, and there is no better place for these. I love watching college sports, and UGA's coaches are some of my best friends.

The next year I had two job offers that I just couldn't pull the trigger on, knowing how hard it would be to start over and rebuild. I got involved with broadcasting and enjoyed staying around the game. People have asked, "Why did you stay in Athens?" It basically boiled down to the quality of life and how special this place is. Visiting friends, teammates, players, and family have always been part of my bucket list.

As I attend the reunions of national championship teams, conference champions, or others that didn't reach these goals, it always makes my ultimate bucket list when these guys start calling me "Coach." I was and still am their coach and am so proud of what they have become and how they represented the different schools when we were together—whether it resulted in a terrific victory or heartbreaking loss.

There are so many places, events, and entertainment choices to enjoy here in Athens. I hope you can check some of these items off your bucket list. Because the people of this area are so genuine, they make those items even more rewarding.

—Jim Donnan
Georgia head coach 1996–2000
Inducted in College Football Hall of Fame in 2009

Introduction

Having grown up right outside of Athens, Georgia, and now as a beat writer for *The Telegraph* in Macon, Georgia, I've seen my entire life what Georgia football has meant to not only the local residents, but also to the more than 100,000 people who are in the Athens vicinity on gamedays. Although Sanford Stadium seats 92,746 people, plenty more hang around just hoping to snag a ticket or to party with their friends before and after the game while catching the day's action on a television at one of the local bars downtown.

Football is the driving force for a lot of people connected to Athens. It's easy to see why, considering Georgia has fielded a football team since 1892, when the entire university was located only on North Campus. The University of Georgia can be viewed as a microcosm of the evolution of college football. At first Georgia played on a field near the university chapel. Then it upgraded to a 30,000-seat stadium. Now, more people fill Sanford Stadium each Saturday than nearly any NFL venue in the country.

Georgia fans live and die with their team. The glory days of the 1980s still ring home for those fortunate enough to have lived through them. The early-to-mid 1990s were forgetful for most until Jim Donnan was hired. Mark Richt then brought even more hope and pride back to the university for 15 years. Now, the Georgia faithful have turned to a new head coach in Kirby Smart to lead the program to even bigger and better things.

Following Georgia doesn't end with the athletics program. Those who attended the University of Georgia tend to develop a deep connection with the city of Athens as well. Football takes up entire Saturdays from pregaming to the actual game to celebrating—or wallowing in misery. Fall Friday nights can be a blast. The music scene in Athens is one of the best of any college town in the nation. There are excellent dining options to socialize with friends. The bar scene is incredible, considering that's basically what downtown Athens thrives on.

Georgia football has a long and storied history that dates back to when Benjamin Harrison was the president of this country. Think about that for a moment. Twenty-three men have sat in the Oval Office since Georgia football played its first game. It's been a long time since the first game at Herty Field saw Georgia wallop Mercer 50–0.

A lot has happened since—both to the game of football and to the city of Athens. Hopefully this book can serve as both a historical account of the UGA football program and as a guide to how to enjoy its peripheries.

THE
GEORGIA BULLDOGS FANS'
BUCKET LIST

Spanning the Eras

Know the Beginnings

To look back at the beginning of Georgia football, one must look up the East Coast to a well-known medical school called Johns Hopkins, which would become well-known as a dominant force in the sport of lacrosse. But a certain person attending Johns Hopkins in the late 1800s helped become the catalyst for the beginning of American football at the University of Georgia.

Dr. Charles Herty was born in Milledgeville, Georgia, on December 4, 1867. He'd stay in the state for his undergraduate academic pursuits in the field of philosophy, electing to attend the University of Georgia. After graduating, Herty pursued his doctorate at Johns Hopkins and concluded it in 1890. When Herty was wrapping up his doctorate in chemistry, Johns Hopkins' upstart football program had been around for nine years.

Herty, who would go on to become an internationally respected chemist, had a long love for athletics. Once his studies were done at Johns Hopkins, Herty moved back to Georgia and served as an assistant chemist at the Georgia Agricultural Experiment Station. By 1891 he was a chemistry instructor at the University of Georgia and spent the next decade in such a role.

This is where his athletic pursuits at UGA began. Although he would become renowned in the field of chemistry for his work in the turpentine and forestry industries, it was what he did in the early 1890s with the Georgia athletics department that is at the top of his legacy at the university. Herty helped organize an athletics agency on campus, which included raising money, forming an intramural sports league, and, most notably, organizing the first football team ever at Georgia. Herty did so and became the coach as well, which gave him the moniker of the "father of Georgia football."

"I'll never forget the first practice," George Shackleford, a football player on that first team, once said. "Dr. Herty simply tossed the football in the air and watched us scramble for it. He selected the strongest looking specimens for the first team."

The first game Georgia ever played, which was on what would be known as Herty Field on North Campus, was against Mercer on January 30, 1892. Georgia won that game in blowout fashion, defeating Mercer 50–0. The next Georgia football game would be set up by Herty and his friend and classmate at Johns Hopkins, Dr. George Petrie, who was at Auburn University. Herty and Petrie set the game up to be played in Atlanta. It would be Georgia's second and Auburn's first, and Auburn won 10–0. That would go down as the first meeting in what's now accurately called "the Deep South's Oldest Rivalry."

Herty would serve as Georgia's football coach for one season, which only consisted of two games. But that would be the start of a long-standing Georgia football career, one that would go from crowds of 2,000 to almost 93,000.

Ernest Brown and Robert Winston coached the Georgia teams in 1893 and 1894, respectively, before a figure, who would go down in fooball lore, came to Athens to coach the university's program. In 1895 and 1896, Glenn "Pop" Warner, who became responsible for a lot of the aspects of the modern game of football, came to Georgia to coach the football team. Among his innovations were the single and double-wing formations, as well as the three-point blocking stance technique. Warner's coaching career began in Georgia for those two years with the then-young head coach compiling a 7–4 record, which included going 4–0 in 1896. Interestingly enough, Warner also coached Iowa State at the same time because the two schools' seasons didn't overlap. After the 4–0 season in 1896, Warner's alma mater at Cornell came calling to bring him back to be its head coach. With two years of overlap at Iowa State still to go, Warner eventually became the head coach at Cornell only in 1904.

A slew of coaches would occupy the head of the football team in years to follow. Charles McCarthy, Gordon Saussy, E.E. Jones, Billy Reynolds, M.M. Dickinson, Charles A. Barnard, W.S. Whitney, Branch

Bocock, J. Coulter, Frank Dobson, and W.A. Cunningham were Georgia coaches from 1897 to 1919. Then Georgia got a coach who would deliver the university its first conference championship.

The turnover rate in coaches was a reflection of the lack of success they were able to have—at least until Cunningham took over in 1910. Although Reynolds went 5–7–3 in two seasons, he was liked among the student body, which gave him a cigar box and a pipe as a parting gift. Barnard, however, was none too liked by his players or Georgia's fans after a 1–5 campaign in 1904.

Cunningham then became Georgia's first coach at the helm for more than two years. He brought respect to the program as the wins began to pile up. Cunningham coached Georgia's first All-American in Bob McWhorter and George "Kid" Woodruff. During 1917 and 1918, Georgia didn't field a football team with World War I going on. Cunningham actually joined the Army during the war before coming back to coach the 1919 season. After compiling a 43–18–9 record over nine seasons, Cunningham re-entered the Army and eventually reached the rank of general.

In 1920 H.J. Stegeman took control and put Georgia at a spot it had never been before. Stegeman, who played college ball for Amos Alonzo Stagg at Chicago, was an assistant under Cunningham before his promotion. It was also during this season when Georgia officially adopted the nickname Bulldogs. The stars aligned, and Georgia went 8–0–1 in Stegeman's first season. It was capped with a Southern Intercollegiate Athletic Association championship. Stegeman coached two more seasons but also coached Georgia's basketball, baseball, and track programs. He remained at Georgia for 18 years as the university's athletic director. Georgia's basketball home, Stegeman Coliseum, is named after him.

Woodruff then took over as Georgia's head coach in 1923 and went 30–16–1 in five years. One of the key elements Woodruff brought to Georgia was the "Box 4 shift" offense. He did so after seeing Notre Dame dismantle Georgia Tech with this style of attack. Woodruff even

The Tragedy of Richard "Von" Gammon

Georgia football was in its infancy—only in its sixth season—when Richard "Von" Gammon was a sophomore. A talented athlete from Rome, Georgia, Gammon was one of Georgia's standout players on its 1897 football team.

Georgia only played three games that season with Virginia being the last. During the game Gammon recorded a tackle on a Virginia player and sustained a serious head injury. When the bodies piled up on the play got up, Gammon remained motionless on the ground. As the story has been told, two doctors attending the game in the stands rushed to his aid. After he was helped to the sideline, Gammon began to throw up before losing consciousness. With the game being played at Piedmont Park in Atlanta, Gammon was rushed to Grady Memorial Hospital.

Unfortunately, Gammon died the next day on October 31, 1897, at the age of 17. A funeral was held the next day at First Presbyterian Church.

In the aftermath Georgia, Georgia Tech, and Mercer stopped playing for the remainder of the year. *The Atlanta Journal* headlined a story on the subject called the "Death Knell of Football." As news spread throughout the state, the Georgia legislature decided to spring into action and crafted a bill to ban football at all statewide public universities. It passed by a vote of 91–3. After also passing in the Georgia

brought in some assistants who coached under Notre Dame's Knute Rockne—Frank Thomas, Harry Mehre, and Jim Crowley—to implement the system. It was not only an introduction of the Box 4 shift to Georgia, but to southeastern football as a whole. Woodruff famously took a salary of only $1 a season due to the money he made in the business arena. Woodruff's 1927 team went 9–1. Georgia was ranked No. 1 entering the final regular-season game against Georgia Tech. But Georgia was upset 12–0, which cost the Bulldogs a chance at an undisputed national championship. Although Georgia still claims a national championship that season because two polls (Boand System, Poling System) ranked it No. 1, Illinois would go on to be the team that historians consider college football's national title team that season. The aforementioned three assistants he brought to coach under him

Senate, all that was needed was for Georgia Governor William Y. Atkinson to sign the bill into law.

Gammon's mother, however, was not in support of this piece of legislation. Rosalind Burns Gammon wrote the following letter to a local representative urging the state lawmakers to not place a ban on the sport her son loved dearly.

> It would be the greatest favor to the family of Von Gammon if your influence could prevent his death being used for an argument detrimental to the athletic cause and its advancement at the University. His love for his college and his interest in all manly sports, without which he deemed the highest type of manhood impossible, is well known by his classmates and friends, and it would be inexpressibly sad to have the cause he held so dear injured by his sacrifice. Grant me the right to request that my boy's death should not be used to defeat the most cherished object of his life. Dr. Herty's article in the Constitution of Nov. 2d is timely, and the authorities of the University can be trusted to make all needed changes for all possible consideration pertaining to the welfare of its students, if they are given the means and the confidence their loyalty and high sense of duty should deserve.

Atkinson was made aware of this letter and vetoed the bill on December 7, 1897.

all became head coaches in their own right. Thomas went on to lead Alabama, and Crowley took the reins at Michigan State.

Mehre, however, became Georgia's head coach after Woodruff stepped down. In his second season in 1929, the same year Sanford Stadium opened up, Mehre's Bulldogs upset Yale 15–0. Famed player Catfish Smith scored each point. Although Mehre never won a conference title, his teams were very much in contention in 1930, 1931, 1933, and 1934. Mehre wound up leaving Georgia to become the head football coach at Ole Miss in 1938 but is still a revered man around Georgia, as his name is part of the Butts-Mehre Heritage Hall that houses the Bulldogs' football program. He compiled a 59–34–6 record during his 10 years in Athens.

With Mehre gone, Georgia hired Joel Hunt to become its 19th football head coach. Maybe it was due to the success Mehre had before him, but the fans and alumni didn't care much for Hunt in what would be his lone season in 1938. Hunt left but saw an assistant he brought along stay behind to follow as Georgia's 20th head football coach.

His name was Wally Butts.

Relax at Herty Field

Named after the football team's first coach, Dr. Charles Herty, Herty Field opened in the fall of 1891 and became the location for the University of Georgia's home games. Located on North Campus, the field was initially used as a marching ground for the university's ROTC. But under Herty's direction, the field became a place for football games and practices, as well as intramural events. It was originally named Alumni Athletic Field.

The first Georgia football game ever played at Herty Field was against Mercer with the then–Red and Black winning by a score of 50–0 on January 30, 1892. Herty Field would be Georgia's home turf when opposing teams came to town to take on the football team until 1911. Named after former Georgia professor, and later president, Steadman Vincent Sanford, Sanford Field was constructed, and Herty Field was converted into a greenspace where students could study, converse,

Though Georgia used to play football here in the early 20th century, Herty Field is now a great place to study, read, and relax. (Jason Butt)

and socialize. Intramural sports teams and the ROTC would still use the field as well.

In the 1940s, however, Herty Field would be no more. The university elected to create the Herty Drive Parking Lot over what was once the football team's home field. It would remain that way for five decades.

But in 1999 Georgia decided to make it a greenspace again, and it's been that way ever since. Located by the Alexander Campbell King Law Library, Herty Field is now a place for students to study, read, and relax. A fountain exists on the site, adding an aesthetic to the

History of North Campus

Herty Field is one of many historical landmarks located at the University of Georgia's North Campus. What's called North Campus now is where the original campus was located. In 1785 the state's general assembly signed an act that granted a state-supported university. It took some time to build, as it wasn't until 1801 that 633 acres of land in Athens were purchased by the soon-to-be university's board of trustees.

The first building to go up was Franklin College, now known as Old College. Built and named to honor Benjamin Franklin, the three-story brick building still stands today and holds classes as part of the Franklin College of Arts and Sciences. It's able to do so thanks to a major 2006 renovation.

The entry to North Campus is landmarked with the famous arch on Broad Street, which has been designed as one of the logos the university uses for promotion. The old superstition is that students are not supposed to walk under the arch until they graduate. Instead, they must walk around it. The arch was cast in the 1800s at the Athens Foundry and was made after the state's seal.

Also on North Campus is The Chapel, which was constructed in 1832. This replaced the original 1807 Chapel that caught fire and was destroyed in 1830. The aesthetics of North Campus provide reminders of the origins of a university that launched the advent of higher public education.

historical site of where the early Georgia football teams used to play. Although the field wasn't as pretty back in those days as it is now, it certainly serves as much more of a reminder of Georgia's football history than a parking lot ever could have.

Become Part of Wally's World

When Joel Hunt came to Georgia, he brought along an unknown assistant named Wally Butts. Hunt only stayed for one season in 1938, a disappointing 5–4–1 campaign. When Hunt left, Georgia turned to Butts to fill the role. As even the Georgia sports communications staff states in its media information, the best thing Hunt did for the Georgia football program was bring Butts along with him to the university.

Butts was born near Milledgeville, Georgia, on February 7, 1905, and excelled in football, basketball, and baseball as a youth. He accepted a scholarship to compete in all three sports at Mercer. He became an All-Southern Conference end in college and quickly became a coach after graduation. He coached at the prep level and only lost 10 games over a decade's worth of time. This helped him become an assistant at Georgia with Hunt bringing him on the staff in 1938.

It wasn't always easy early on. The one the fans began to call the "Little Round Man" had a tough go at it in his attempt to rebuild the football team into a regional and national power. In his first season, Butts, who also became Georgia's athletic director in his inaugural season, led the Bulldogs to a 5–6 record.

Butts would endure another tough season in year two, though it ended over .500. In 1940 his team finished 5–4–1 with wins against Georgia Tech and Miami to close the year. From there, Butts had the Georgia machine rolling.

His 1941 team, featuring Frank Sinkwich at halfback, steamrolled opponents to a 9–1–1 record. Butts' offense was quite prolific, featuring an 81–0 win against Mercer, a 34–6 win against South Carolina and a 35–0 win against Dartmouth. Butts was renowned for being a coaching genius who would do what it took to win ballgames. His teams played with the kind of tenacity he'd exhibit in practice and on the sidelines in games. At the end of the 1941 season, Butts' team played in its first bowl game, the 1942 Orange Bowl, which saw the Bulldogs defeat TCU 40–26. That set the stage for a big 1942 season, one that Georgia fans, old and new alike, reflect upon fondly. The Bulldogs jumped out to a 9–0 start, which featured a 75–0 throttling against Florida. To date, that's still the largest margin of victory seen in the longstanding rivalry between the Bulldogs and Gators.

Butts' Bulldogs, however, dropped a 27–13 game against Auburn that kept them from being unblemished that season. Still, Georgia went on to finish 11–1 thanks to the tandem of Sinkwich and Charley Trippi. Sinkwich would become Georgia's first ever Heisman Trophy winner in 1942, one year after he was a Heisman finalist. After beating Georgia Tech 34–0 in the season finale, the Bulldogs would go on to defeat UCLA 9–0 in the Rose Bowl.

The strong finish after the Auburn loss placed Georgia No. 1 in more than half of the polls at the time. Therefore, plenty of historians who look back on this particular season consider Georgia the 1942 consensus national champion, even though Ohio State finished No. 1 in the AP poll. In those days the final AP poll came out before bowl games, and the Buckeyes did not participate in a bowl that year. To celebrate Butts' championship at Georgia, the Bulldogs fly a 1942 national champion banner at Sanford Stadium.

Butts was a bit of an innovator during his day. Not too many teams nationally cared much about the forward pass. It was all about running off tackle and getting into Saturday slugfests. As a senior in 1942, however, Sinkwich threw for a then-SEC record of 1,392 yards, which stood for eight years. Butts was big on running the ball as well but didn't believe you should shun the pass since it was an available method to move the ball.

When the United States entered World War II, the country asked a lot of young men to fight. This forced a lot of Butts' players to leave the team. So it wouldn't be until 1946 when Georgia would dominate the SEC again. With Trippi back on board and captaining that team, the Bulldogs put together their first ever perfect full season (not counting the 4–0–0 campaign of 1896). The closest any team got that season was in a November 2, 1946 game against Alabama with the Bulldogs winning 14–0. In the Sugar Bowl, Georgia defeated North Carolina 20–10 to cap the perfect campaign. But every poll except one decided not to crown Georgia the national champion. Despite a mid-season tie against Army, Notre Dame earned the consensus national championship for the season. Georgia finished No. 1 in the Williamson Poll with the school claiming that season as a national championship campaign while recognizing it's not of the consensus variety.

Butts was a dominating coach in the 1940s. His Georgia teams combined for a 78–27–4 record over that particular decade, including a consensus national championship, a claimed national championship, and three SEC championships with the third coming in a 9–2 campaign in 1948.

The 1950s, however, weren't as kind to Butts. The 1953 season saw Georgia go 3–8 with the Bulldogs posting four consecutive losing seasons from 1955 to 1958. Butts and the Bulldogs would bounce back in 1959 with an SEC championship, finishing 10–1 and a perfect 7–0 record in conference play. Quarterback Fran Tarkenton was on the 1959 team and still holds fond memories of Butts as a head coach. "I was fascinated every day at practice with his schemes and passing drills," Tarkenton said. "I was intrigued with his knowledge of the passing game."

In 1960 Butts' Bulldogs finished 6–4, and the fanbase and alumni became a tad restless. Butts was allowed to resign as head coach and to retain his athletic director title. But the end of his tenure at Georgia was one brought upon by scandal, which ended up in his favor in the long run in the court of law.

The Saturday Evening Post wrote a story headlined "The Story of a College Football Fix," which told the tale of Butts and Alabama head coach Paul "Bear" Bryant conspiring with one another to give the Crimson Tide an advantage during the two teams' 1962 game. As the story was written, an insurance salesman named George Burnett was phoning a local public relations firm. Allegedly, phone lines were crossed, and Burnett happened to be connected to a phone call between Butts and Bryant with Butts giving Bryant detailed information about Georgia's gameplan going into that week's game against Alabama. Although the Crimson Tide were a 14-to-17-point favorite, they won 35–0. As word of this allegation trickled to Georgia officials, Butts was questioned over the accusation. He would later resign in 1963, stating the decision was due to "purely personal and business reasons."

The accusation in the story most certainly wouldn't be the end of it. Butts sued *The Saturday Evening Post*'s owner, Curtis Publishing Company, in what would become a landmark libel case. During the trial three Georgia players and three Alabama players testified that they didn't believe Alabama held any of Georgia's gameplan information or plays prior to the game taking place. Butts and Bryant acknowledged a call took place but said no strategic information on that game was shared. Perhaps the biggest bombshell at the trial was the fact *The Saturday Evening Post* did not review the notes Burnett claimed to have taken while listening in on the call. A jury didn't take long to vindicate Butts, awarding him $60,000 in general damages and a staggering $3 million in punitive damages. The case would be appealed all the way to the U.S. Supreme Court with Butts winning each appellate decision. Butts' $3 million award was later reduced to $460,000. More importantly, Butts' name was cleared by the legal system in what otherwise was an astonishing accusation. The case went on to establish libel law for public figures vs. public officials.

Although Butts resigned as Georgia's athletic director in 1963, the Bulldogs honored his legacy at the university by naming the football team's complex in his honor. Butts-Mehre Heritage Hall—named after Butts and former head coach Harry Mehre—was dedicated in 1987. When walking into the building, you will see two busts of Butts and Mehre at the front entrance.

Butts finished his career at Georgia 140–86–9. It's the third best win total in a Georgia coaching career behind Vince Dooley and Mark Richt. Butts was elected to the Georgia Sports Hall of Fame in 1966 and to the College Football Hall of Fame in 1997. Butts died at the age of 68 on December 17, 1973.

Visit Butts-Mehre Heritage Hall

What Georgia fan wouldn't want to walk through a Georgia football and athletics museum? If you're in Athens, Georgia, definitely stop by Butts-Mehre Heritage Hall, the complex where the Georgia football coaching staff works and operates. Although visitors are not allowed to go to see the coaching staff—obviously—it's basically a treasure for anyone who wants to relive the past achievements of the Georgia football program.

Located at 1 Selig Circle, off of Lumpkin Street and behind the Spec Towns outdoor track, Butts-Mehre Heritage Hall is a 138,000-square foot building that overlooks outdoor practice fields and is now adjacent to an indoor practice facility, which finished construction and was opened for full use in January of 2017. The building is named after former football coaches Wally Butts and Harry Mehre.

The UGA sports museum features the best of the past of Georgia athletics. In the lobby entrance located on the third floor of the building, you can see the four jerseys—Frank Sinkwich, Charley Trippi, Theron Sapp, and Herschel Walker—the university has retired. There are other exhibits on the third floor featuring highlights and achievements honored in other sports such as basketball, track and field, baseball, and softball. Either an elevator ride or walk down a flight of stairs to

Butts-Mehre Heritage Hall, the 138,000-square foot complex where the Georgia football coaches work, also houses a sports museum. (Jason Butt)

the second floor continues the museum with Georgia's bowl trophies on display for all to see. In addition, there are interactive displays visitors can watch and listen to, which feature some of Georgia's most famous football plays on screen with the accompanying radio call from Larry Munson, the longtime voice of the Bulldogs. Among those is the famous "Run, Lindsay, Run!" call, which came when Lindsay Scott scored a 93-yard catch-and-run touchdown to beat Florida in 1980.

The first floor is off limits to visitors since that's where the football team does most of its work. On that level is a weight room, sports medicine room, equipment room, and meeting rooms for the players.

Butts-Mehre Heritage Hall is open Monday through Friday from 8:00 AM until 5:00 PM. Visitors are welcome during this time to peruse the Georgia exhibits in the areas designed for the public.

Go Between the Hedges

When describing a Georgia football game, it is often referred to as taking place "between the hedges." Those hedges, which enclose the football field at Sanford Stadium, have become hallowed due to the long history that they've been there for. In fact, ever since Sanford Stadium was built in 1929, the hedges have been there.

Interestingly enough, the hedges weren't intended to be hedges. The original idea came from Charlie E. Martin, a business manager in Georgia's athletics department. As legend has it, per former sports information director/tennis coach/team historian Dan Magill and via the *Athens Banner-Herald,* Martin attended a Rose Bowl in Pasadena, California, and became enamored with a hedge of roses. He wanted to enclose Sanford Stadium with them and approached Georgia's horticulturists about it.

The horticulturists, however, told Martin that the weather in Georgia would not support the hedge of roses. Therefore, they suggested going with a hedge of *privet ligustrum.* This genus has served as Georgia's hedges ever since. The hedges were only one foot high when planted in time for Georgia's first game at Sanford Stadium—a 15–0 victory against Yale. They were also protected by a wooden fence. Planting the hedges proved more difficult than originally thought. Opting to go with the *privet ligustrum* was a last-minute decision. It turned into a late-night/early-morning affair to transport the hedges from Atlanta and dig into the field just in time before kickoff of the Georgia-Yale game. Georgia's crew was able to get the job done as 30,000 fans came to that inaugural game at Sanford Stadium, which was the largest crowd for a southern college football game at the time.

The hedges are now roughly five feet tall, and each box is about five feet wide. The hedges are what separate the now much larger Sanford Stadium—of more than 92,000 people—from the football field. The hedges have become one of the top traditions in Georgia football history.

And since Georgia fans revere the hedges so much, they have become a target from other programs. It seems whenever Georgia Tech defeats Georgia at Sanford Stadium, the Yellow Jacket players take pieces of the hedges with them. When Georgia Tech snapped a seven-game losing streak against Georgia with a win at Sanford Stadium in 2008, the visiting team's locker room was littered with hedges. The same occurred in 2014 and 2016. Teams such as Auburn and Tennessee have also been known to take a branch or two if they win at Sanford Stadium.

Nick Chubb runs past the famed hedges of Sanford Stadium while scoring a touchdown in 2014. (AP Images)

The *privet ligustrum* may be sacred to UGA, but it's a weed to everyone else. And since it is as such, great care must be taken to keep its shape and to protect it from disease. In 1996, when Atlanta hosted the Summer Olympics, Sanford Stadium was the venue for women's soccer. Since the dimension for a soccer field is bigger than a football field, the hedges needed to come out.

This enraged the football faithful at the time, considering it blasphemous to remove the storied hedges from Sanford Stadium. As it turned out, the hedges were dealing with nematodes, which made the removal surprisingly timely. Once the Olympics were over, Georgia used healthy parts of the hedges to create the new and improved border around the stadium.

There have been some humorous times involving the hedges, too. One in particular came in a 2011 Georgia football game against New Mexico State. Former tight end Aron White caught a touchdown from quarterback Aaron Murray. His momentum, however, carried him toward a couple of xylophones the Redcoat Band had next to the hedges. Trying to avoid the xylophones, White jumped in the air and into the hedges. White's jersey got stuck, and multiple teammates had to run over to help get him out.

When he finally became untangled, the Sanford Stadium crowd erupted in celebration. The hedges served as no joke as White suffered a bruised knee as well as other minor injuries after the fall. "I was more worried about the xylophones, I was like, 'Man, this thing is metal, it's gonna hurt,'" White told reporters after the game. "As soon as I saw it, it was a reflex to jump over it. And then once I actually hit the hedges, that first branch hit me, and I was like, 'This is not soft!' It's not like a little soft bush. It's a prickly, man, it's hard. It hurt. Branches were snapping and cracking, and I was just like, 'Man.' Once I hit the bottom, stuff was poking me, man. I couldn't even see straight. My helmet was kind of twisted. Nobody helped me up, and I couldn't get up. It was a little traumatic out there, I'm not going to lie. I was freaked out a little bit, maybe. But my boys got me out of there.

It's a funny memory, man, my first touchdown in Sanford. I'm glad it was a memorable one."

The landscaping crew tended to the affected area and saw a sizable branch broken off of it. A member of the crew gave White the branch, which he kept as a souvenir.

Legend has it that Atlanta-based sportswriter Grantland Rice coined the term "between the hedges" to reference a Georgia football game. The phrase certainly applies. Using plenty of diligence to ensure the hedges are intact, including a surveillance system to protect against intruders, the hedges are quite sacred to Georgia's football program. Initially expected to be roses, the green weed has long served as the barrier for many memories on the storied grounds of Sanford Stadium.

Learn the Evolution of Sanford Stadium

There's an old saying for Saturdays at Sanford Stadium, which is that there's nothing better than spending time with 92,000 of your closest friends. Georgia's home stadium officially seats 92,746 people, which makes for quite the atmosphere on gamedays. Much like other schools in the Southeast, college football is practically a religion with Sanford Stadium being the place of worship.

Like anything, there was a long evolutionary period for the stadium to become what it is today. The first location Georgia played games at was Herty Field, which is located on what's now considered North Campus. From 1892 to 1911, Georgia held its home games at Herty before moving to Sanford Field, which was named after former professor Steadman Vincent Sanford, who later became the university's president. Sanford Field was located on Lumpkin Street and had wooden bleachers for seating. It stood as Georgia's home field for 19 years. In 1929 Georgia constructed Sanford Stadium, which was built nearby and still stands at its present location.

The construction for the stadium cost a whopping $360,000—a ton of money in those days—with the venue seating approximately 30,000 people.

The first two games of the 1929 season saw Georgia host Oglethorpe and Furman at Sanford Field with the Bulldogs going 1–1 to start. The third week of the season saw the opening of Sanford Stadium with mighty Yale coming to town. It turned out to be one to remember as Georgia pulled off the home upset 15–0 in head coach Harry Mehre's second season.

Sanford Stadium's next move would be to add lights to the field level in 1940 so that the team could play at night. The first night game ever played at Sanford Stadium was against Kentucky on October 25, 1940, which ended in a 7–7 tie. In 1949 6,000 seats were added to the south stands of the stadium, marking the first expansion since it opened. Fifteen years later in 1964, which marked the first season head coach Vince Dooley took over the team, the university would add 7,621 seats to the end zone, bringing the seating capacity to 43,621. But in doing so, lights were removed from the field level of the stadium. Three years after that in 1967, Sanford Stadium would undergo its first dramatic transformation. The university added an upper level to the stadium, which added 19,640 seats. The total cost for this was $3 million with club seating, a press box, and a president's box being added as well. After this renovation Sanford Stadium housed 59,000 people on gamedays.

The next major construction came in 1981 when Georgia had the Sanford Stadium east end zone enclosed. That added 19,000 additional seats, which brought the capacity up to 82,122. This construction cost the university $11.5 million. A year later in 1982, Georgia installed lights with 12 poles, which included 420 metal bulbs. In 1984 the Letterman's Club was added on the east end of the stadium, which was a 5,460 square-foot addition to Sanford Stadium.

In 1991 Georgia enclosed the west end of Sanford Stadium, which added 4,205 seats. This brought the seating capacity up to 85,434. In

1994 Georgia constructed 30 SkySuites, and 20 more were added six years later in 2000. The total cost for those additions came to more than $18 million. The first addition made the seating capacity 86,117 with the second bringing the total to 86,520.

In 2003 Georgia added 5,500 seats to the second upper deck on the north side of the stadium. This $25 million job brought Sanford Stadium's capacity to 92,058. And finally, in 2004, Georgia added the North Side SkySuites, which added 688 seats, bringing Sanford Stadium's capacity to what it is today—92,746.

A lot of work, and almost $71 million that we know about, has gone into bringing Sanford Stadium into the venue it is today. And so many events and memories have been had between the hedges. Oh, and in case you were wondering, those famed hedges have been there since the beginning—when Georgia upset Yale 15–0 in 1929.

Reminisce About the Dooley Days

He was only 31 years old and had no varsity head coaching experience. It's easy to look back and see why Georgia fans were hesitant at embracing the new ball coach right away when he was brought on board. But then-athletic director Joel Eaves believed in Vince Dooley, an assistant and freshman team football coach at Auburn. Looking back, especially in today's era, it would seem like hiring someone that young and with such little experience to lead a football team was quite risky. But after looking at what transpired during Dooley's time as Georgia's head football coach, it certainly proved to be the correct decision.

Although no one in Athens knew anything about Dooley, Eaves did. Eaves spent 15 years as Auburn's head basketball coach and was familiar enough with Dooley as a football coach to see the potential he had. In hindsight Dooley, who would go on to follow Eaves as Georgia's athletic director, is amazed he got the job at such a young age. But Eaves had a feeling the young up-and-comer could turn Georgia's fortunes around. The Bulldogs were coming off of three substandard seasons under head coach Johnny Griffith.

Dooley was born on September 4, 1932, in Mobile, Alabama, and grew up starring in both football and basketball. Basketball was actually considered his better sport. But an injury affected his basketball career, and Dooley only played football at Auburn. Graduating from The Plains after the 1953 season, Dooley became an assistant football coach at Auburn just a couple of years later. Coaching the freshman team in his mid-20s, Dooley earned some valuable management experience that he could carry over when his big break eventually came.

The first game Dooley coached didn't go too well. In the season opener, he was inside Denny Stadium taking on the Bear Bryant-coached Alabama Crimson Tide. Alabama moved up and down the field all day and defeated Georgia 31–3. Dooley's first team would win two of its next three games sandwiched around a tie. The Bulldogs then lost a hard-fought game against No. 10 Florida State, which signaled Dooley had this team headed in the right direction. Georgia won five of its last six, which included wins against Florida and Georgia Tech and then against Texas Tech in the Sun Bowl. It was the first time a Georgia team had won seven games in five years.

Dooley would continue to rebuild the program in 1965 with Georgia finishing 6–4. But the Bulldogs recorded a season-opening 18–17 win against Alabama and scored a 15–7 win against Michigan. But losses to Florida State, Kentucky, Florida, and Auburn put a damper on a season that started with three consecutive wins.

Dooley's breakthrough came in his third year. The Bulldogs recorded four wins to start the year before succumbing to a tough 7–6 loss to Miami. From there Georgia wouldn't lose, recording wins against rivals Florida, Auburn, and Georgia Tech. That earned the Bulldogs a Cotton Bowl berth against SMU with Georgia winning 24–9. Georgia would finish No. 4 in both of the AP and coaches' polls. In three years Dooley took a struggling team and placed it in the top five nationally.

In Dooley's first 16 seasons, his teams won three SEC championships in 1966, 1968, and 1976. Dooley's team in 1968 finished first in the final Litkenhous poll, which allowed Georgia to acknowledge a national championship season without formally claiming it. Dooley had done wonders with the program and offered the kind of consistency it so badly needed. But Dooley would take the Dogs to heights they'd never seen before during the 1980s.

Of course, a lot of that had to do with a certain running back named Herschel Walker, whom he recruited. In those days, coaches could "bump" into recruits on the trail, and Dooley ensured that either he or an assistant would be around to check in on Walker when the staff was legally able to per NCAA rules. Dooley didn't want to start Walker right away in the 1980 season opener against Tennessee. Walker was just a freshman and hadn't done anything too spectacular in practices leading up to the game. But Georgia trailed 9–0 and needed a spark. Dooley was talked into turning to Walker in the second half, which turned out to be the best decision of the day. Walker ran through Tennessee safety Bill Bates to cut Tennessee's lead to 15–9. Walker would score a later touchdown to give Georgia a 16–15 win.

That 1980 season played out magnificently for Georgia. The Bulldogs went undefeated and took care of business in most games. There were a couple of close ones—a 13–10 win against George Rogers and the South Carolina Gamecocks, and, of course, the 26–21 win against Florida that saw Buck Belue hit Lindsay Scott for a 93-yard touchdown late in the game. But not too long after Georgia defeated Georgia Tech, Dooley became linked to the Auburn job. Dooley's alma mater made a serious run at him and offered a contract that would have been worth $1.8 million. The Tigers wanted to bring Dooley home, and a lot of people thought it would happen. Georgia's assistants were doing what they could to ensure defensive coordinator Erk Russell would serve as the head coach for the Sugar Bowl against Notre Dame while getting the job full time for the following year.

But after three days, Dooley decided against taking the Auburn job. His roots were in Georgia after 17 years. He stuck with Georgia, even though the fact he went to college and played at Auburn weighed heavily on his mind. "I knew it was a tremendous opportunity," Dooley said. "Auburn was ripe at the time. That entered into my thinking. I knew it was going to be a good situation; maybe it was time to leave. I'd been here a long time. As I thought about the positive parts, they were strong enough to make me really interested. But I never got to the point where I said, 'Yeah, I'm going to do it.'"

Dooley got back to work and coached his No. 1 Georgia squad against No. 7 Notre Dame. The Bulldogs would win 17–10 and carry their head coach off of the field. That championship would start a wild run for Georgia. The Bulldogs would win a total of three consecutive SEC championships from 1980 to 1982. Walker would win the Heisman Trophy in 1982. Georgia would add a 10-win season in 1983 and consecutive nine-win campaigns to close out his coaching career in 1987 and 1988. As Georgia's head coach, he finished with a career record of 201–77–10.

When Dooley was done with coaching, he remained on as Georgia's athletic director, a position he held beginning in 1979. One of the first things Dooley did was hire Andy Landers to become Georgia's first full-time women's basketball head coach. He helped ensure upgrades to women's sports programs to make the athletics department compliant with the federal government's Title IX legislation. Dooley hired Suzanne Yoculan to lead the Georgia gymnastics team, and she turned that squad into one of the most successful teams in the entire athletic department's history. Although Dooley had to hire and fire both Ray Goff and Jim Donnan, he also hired Mark Richt in December of 2000, and Richt went on to a have a pretty good 15-year run as Georgia's head football coach.

But in that same year of 2000, Dooley was hoping for a contract extension from then-university president Michael Adams. Instead, when the topic was discussed, Adams declined to offer one. Recalling the conversation with Adams, Dooley said the former UGA president offered a backhanded compliment in regards to where he stood. "He said, 'You've done a good job here, Vince, but you never wanted to

DOOLEY'S SUCCESSORS

When it was time for Vince Dooley to step down as Georgia's head coach, he wanted to pass the torch to his assistant and former quarterback, Ray Goff. Georgia's quarterback from 1974 to 1976, Goff helped lead the Bulldogs to an SEC championship in 1976, the same year he was named the conference's Player of the Year. Three years after his college career ended, Goff became an assistant coach at South Carolina before returning to coach under Dooley in 1981.

A running backs coach, Goff also was Georgia's recruiting coordinator in the 1980s and helped bring in some great talent to the roster. Goff's first two seasons finished 6–6 and 4–7, and therefore there wasn't a whole lot to be excited about. But in 1991 Georgia went 9–3 with wins against Auburn and Georgia Tech to close the regular season. The Bulldogs then defeated Arkansas in the Independence Bowl.

A year later in 1992, Georgia went 10–2, and running back Garrison Hearst earned an invitation to the Downtown Athletic Club for the Heisman Trophy ceremony. He finished third in the voting. However, wins didn't materialize over Goff's final three years, as he totaled a 17-16–1 record during that time span. Dooley, as Georgia's athletic director, made the tough decision to fire his former quarterback and assistant, stating that coaching decision was "the most difficult one."

In searching for a new football coach after the 1995 season, Dooley reached an agreement with Glen Mason to replace Goff. Mason was the coach at Kansas and guided the Jayhawks to a 9–2 record in the regular season. But after taking the job, Mason had a change of heart and backed out of the deal. Dooley resumed his coaching search and decided on Marshall head coach Jim Donnan as Goff's replacement.

There was some risk to Donnan since he hadn't been a head coach at a Division I-A program before. But at Marshall, Donnan's teams were always in contention for the Division I-AA playoffs. His Thundering Herd won the 1992 1-AA national championship and played in three other title games in 1991, 1993, and 1995.

The yearly records at Georgia certainly improved under Donnan. After a 5–6 year in 1996, Georgia went 10–2 in 1997, which included a win against Florida. The Bulldogs went 9–3 in 1998, 8–4 in 1999, and 8–4 in 2000. His progress at Georgia caught other programs' attention. He turned down lucrative offers from Oklahoma, North Carolina, and North Carolina State to keep building at Georgia. But what lacked were wins against Georgia's rivals. Donnan went 1–4 against Florida, 1–4 against Tennessee, 2–3 against Georgia Tech, and 2–3 against Auburn. The three losses to Georgia Tech came in consecutive years from 1998 to 2000. Ultimately, it became UGA president Michael Adams' call in the end. Dooley somewhat reluctantly agreed to make a move. "It's something we can't ignore," Dooley said at the time, while adding he initially wanted to give Donnan another year. "Suppose we had a winning record against all four of those teams. Would we be here? The fact of the matter is we would not be here if that was the case."

stay too long. And you need to have something named after you,'" Dooley wrote in his book, *Vince Dooley's Tales from the 1980 Season*.

Three years later, Dooley broached the subject again and was turned away. That set up Dooley's retirement as Georgia's athletic director in 2004. Dooley is still living in Athens and is very much a fan of the Georgia football program. When Richt was let go by current athletic director Greg McGarity, Dooley was present for the news conference and then faced a horde of reporters as if he was coming out of retirement to coach again.

Dooley is a legend around Athens and is immortalized through a statue overlooking the Dooley Sculpture Garden. The statue depicts Dooley being carried off the field on his players' shoulders after the 1981 Sugar Bowl win against Notre Dame. Dooley may have arrived at Georgia as an unknown coach who did not have the kind of experiences first-time head coaches in major conferences generally come in with. But Dooley learned the trade and crafted the Georgia program into a consistent winner. And through his 25-year career as a head football coach, he was able to go out with a coveted national championship, which is something not many football coaches get to claim.

Respect the Richt Era

The 1990s weren't the kindest to Georgia. And therefore, the Bulldogs were looking for a new coach who could bring the needed energy to become a major player in the SEC. About five hours south of Athens, Georgia, in Tallahassee, Florida, a young up-and-coming offensive coordinator was beginning to become a household name in his own right. Mark Richt had coordinated offenses at Florida State during two national championship seasons in 1993 and 1999.

Richt had seen a great deal of success but had been with the Seminoles for 11 seasons. With Florida State poised to play Oklahoma in another national championship game following the 2000 regular season, Richt was approached with the chance to take over Georgia, a team coming off of a 7–4 regular season (it finished 8–4 after beating Virginia in the Oahu Classic but had lost to Georgia Tech for three consecutive seasons).

As Richt said in the moment, it was the kind of job he'd long thought of taking. Once offered it by athletic director Vince Dooley, Richt accepted. "I've had some opportunities over the years, but when I found out that I was a possible candidate for this job, it was the very first time that I got really excited and eager about the possibility of making a move," Richt said.

After Dooley retired from coaching following the 1988 season, Georgia football had been very hit or miss. From 1989 through 2000, the Bulldogs were a combined 86–53–1. Sure, the Bulldogs won their share of games. But by no means were they an SEC powerhouse. Georgia had yet to go to an SEC championship and only recorded two 10-win seasons—one under Ray Goff and one under Jim Donnan.

Otherwise, that wasn't something common in Athens.

So Georgia, with Dooley and then-university president Michael Adams agreeing on the hire, was hopeful Richt could be the one to take the Bulldogs to bigger things. It wouldn't take long for Richt to prove his worth as the right hire at the right time despite not having any previous head coaching experience.

Consider his 2001 season an adjustment year, in which Richt led the Bulldogs to an 8–4 record with a loss in to Boston College in the Music City Bowl. In year two, however, Richt put in one of the best regular seasons in program history. He lit a fire into the program by leading the Bulldogs to an 8–0 start before falling to Florida 20–13. But from there the Bulldogs would win out and win their first ever SEC Championship Game appearance against Arkansas 30–3.

With Miami and Ohio State both finishing the regular season undefeated, Georgia ended the regular season ranked No. 3 and was unable to play for a national championship. The Bulldogs would head to New Orleans and defeat Richt's old team, Florida State, 26–13 in the Sugar Bowl.

This team would go down as one of Richt's better teams, considering the kind of talent that helped put Georgia back on the national stage. David Greene as a sophomore threw for 2,924 yards, 22 touchdowns, and eight interceptions. Musa Smith had a great year running the ball and totaled 1,324 rushing yards and eight touchdowns. Receiver

Terrence Edwards caught 59 passes and recorded Georgia's only 1,000-yard season in program history through the 2016 year with 1,004 yards and 11 touchdowns. It was a special team that won Georgia's first SEC championship in 20 years.

More success would come under Richt's leadership as well. A year later, Georgia would be back in the SEC championship but would lose to LSU. After a 10–2 season in 2004, the Bulldogs would win their second SEC title in four years with Georgia defeating LSU 34–14. Led by D.J. Shockley, Thomas Brown, and Greg Blue, this Georgia team was a formidable foe every week it took the field. But two losses during the regular season would keep the Bulldogs out of the BCS national championship picture, though they still made the Sugar Bowl.

However, that Sugar Bowl didn't go too well as Rich Rodriguez's West Virginia Mountaineers stunned Georgia with its high-octane spread offense. Jumping out to an early four-touchdown lead, Georgia was unable to cap off a rally and fell 38–35.

But Richt and the Bulldogs had plenty to be proud of after this season. It was the first time since 1980 through 1983 that Georgia had posted four consecutive 10-win seasons. The Bulldogs were back in the national conversation and winning a ton of games with Richt as their head coach. Times were good again in Athens with the Bulldogs doing their part to be nationally competitive for a rabid fanbase, and they were selling out Sanford Stadium each Saturday.

Two years later in 2007, Georgia headed back to the Sugar Bowl, and this time pummeled Hawaii 41–10. But it was under disappointing circumstances. After Georgia dropped two games to South Carolina and Tennessee, the Bulldogs reeled off six wins in a row to close the regular season. But having lost the tiebreaker to Tennessee, the Volunteers won the SEC East and played LSU in the conference championship.

In the final week before bowl selection, Georgia was ranked fourth nationally. The top two teams, Missouri and West Virginia, both lost, setting up what could have potentially been a move into the top two by Georgia. But since LSU played for the SEC title and defeated

Tennessee, the pollsters moved the Tigers ahead with the BCS computers ultimately jumping them from No. 7 to No. 2 and into a matchup against Ohio State. LSU would go on and win a national championship while Georgia got the Sugar Bowl win against Hawaii.

With junior quarterback Matthew Stafford and running back Knowshon Moreno, Georgia opened the subsequent season as the preseason No. 1 team. But after a 4–0 start, the Bulldogs lost to Alabama 41–30. After two more losses, Georgia finished 10–3 with a Capital One Bowl victory against Michigan State. A lot of people point to this season as being the beginning of the end of Richt's tenure.

From 2009 to 2015, Richt's teams played in two SEC championships but lost both. Although the 2011 championship game loss to LSU was a blowout, a loss was expected. However, the 2012 loss continues to sting. Facing Alabama with a berth to the BCS national championship on the line, Richt's team played about as good of a game as it possibly could have against the dominant team of its day. Both teams endured a slugfest against each other with Georgia holding a 21–10 lead in the third quarter. But Alabama would mount a furious comeback with the two squads exchanging body blow after body blow in the fourth quarter. Down 32–28 quarterback Aaron Murray led his team down the field with a chance to win the game. After hitting tight end Arthur Lynch for a 26-yard gain to the Alabama 8-yard line, Murray was told to hurry up to the line and run a play. Georgia's coaches didn't want to give Alabama time to substitute its personnel, which is why the offense hurried to the line to run a play instead of spiking the ball. The ball was snapped, and the play was for Murray to throw a back shoulder fade to receiver Malcolm Mitchell. But Alabama linebacker C.J. Mosley tipped the ball, which caused it to fall right into receiver Chris Conley's hands at the 5-yard line. Instinctively, Conley caught the ball but slipped to the Georgia Dome turf. The clock ran out, and Alabama went on to win the national championship a month later over Notre Dame.

It turned out to be one of the more defining moments of Richt's tenure as Georgia's head coach. If he won that game, the Bulldogs would have had a very good chance to go on and beat Notre Dame in the BCS national championship. And if that had been the case, Richt would have likely ended up as the head coach for life at Georgia.

That would turn out not to be the case. Although Richt would still coach the Bulldogs for the next three seasons, he became defined as a coach who, over the latter half of his tenure, couldn't get the program over the proverbial hump. Yes, Richt would go on to post the best winning percentage for any coach in program history. But his career record against Florida by the end of the 2015 season was 5–10. He'd only won two SEC titles in 15 years with the second one coming in 2005.

After losing to Alabama, Tennessee, and Florida in 2015, there were rumblings that a coaching change would be made. Following Georgia's win against Georgia Tech, athletic director Greg McGarity made the call to fire Richt as the program's head coach. "It's part of the business," Richt said. "It's not all that shocking to think that it could happen. My focus was always on moving forward and recruiting and bringing in the best class we could bring in and continue to build a future team that would be able to win a championship. But it didn't work out that way. I guess it's a lot like how I manage things in the middle of a game. If things don't always go exactly the way you want, and you know they don't always go the way you want, you can spend a lot of time to figure out what happened and who did what, or you can figure out where you're at in terms of what do we do next to win. Instead of trying to find a kid that made a mistake or trying to find the coach that did something he shouldn't have done, or maybe he's responsible for something, you want to chew somebody's rear end. My focus has always been on where are we and what do we have to do to win. I feel like the same way right now. I see where I am, Georgia sees where they are, and everybody's going to do what they think is in the best interest to have success in the future, so that's how I look at it."

Richt's tenure at Georgia concluded with a 145–51 record. He's the second-winningest head coach in Georgia history behind Dooley, the man who hired him. His .740 winning percentage is the best Georgia has ever seen. Richt will forever be remembered as a head coach who did things the right way when it came to the profession. His players adored him well after their playing careers were over because of how he treated them while they were at Georgia. "It was tough when I first heard the news," Shockley said. "A little disappointed, a little angry, I had different emotions. He's a guy who has done so much for me and for the university and other guys that came in under him. It's tough to see a guy so consistent—and I know he didn't win the big game everyone wanted—but I thought they would give him at least another year to figure it out. It was a little disappointing."

But that comes with the territory of college football. Even those who succeed in the profession aren't immune to change. And with Richt, his legacy will forever be a great one at Georgia. It just couldn't continue longer than the 15 years it did. "I think that 15 years is a long time," Richt said. "The expectations have been built to the point where if you don't win a championship, it's kind of miserable around here. When we don't make it to Atlanta, I'm miserable, too. I respect our fans, I love our fans. I respect the media, I love a couple of people in the media. I really, I love everybody, quite frankly. I know everybody's got a job to do. Our sport is a very passionate sport, and it's a very public sport. The jobs that we do, everybody seems to have an opinion on it. You can't have all the excitement and the cheering and all that without the other. If things don't go the way people want them to go, I can understand them being disappointed. I can understand them thinking there's a better way and that kind of thing. I respect that. It got to the point where there wasn't enough confidence that my leadership could get it done. That's the prerogative of the people in charge, and I understand that."

Get Excited About Smart's Homecoming

Georgia couldn't replace a legendary coach of 15 years with just anybody. There was a thought inside the program, and among those who play a major role from the outside, that Georgia's 26th head coach would have to be someone who could move the Bulldogs to the kind of heights they saw during the early 1980s.

There was plenty of fixation on a certain assistant coach who played a major role in the rise of Alabama under head coach Nick Saban, as the Crimson Tide established themselves as one of the greatest dynasties in college football history. Alongside Saban for nine years was Kirby Smart, who came to Alabama in 2007 and helped run some of the most dominant defenses in modern history.

Not only was Smart's pedigree as a coach impressive, but he also had ties to Georgia, considering the school was his alma mater and where he played football. After redshirting in 1994, Smart played defensive back from 1995 to 1998, where he asserted himself as a team leader. Those who were close to Smart then knew he'd one day become a coach. But to even be in the consideration of coaching the program he once played for was something that brought tears to his eyes during his introductory news conference on December 7, 2015. "I waited on a great opportunity, which is here at the University of Georgia right now," Smart said. "No better place in the country to be—one of the top programs in the country, top storied programs, very fertile recruiting ground, very supportive administration."

Smart was calculated throughout his coaching career. Once it became clear he wasn't going to play in the NFL after his college career was over, Smart became an administrative assistant at Georgia in 1999. Smart then spent two years coaching Valdosta State under head coach Chris Hatcher. A funny story emerged that Smart diagramed a defensive play during his interview featuring only 10 men on the field. He still got the job and parlayed that into an graduate assistant opportunity under Bobby Bowden at Florida State.

Two seasons passed, and Smart became the defensive backs coach under Nick Saban in 2004 at LSU. After just one season, Smart came back to Georgia in 2005 and coached running backs on Richt's SEC championship team. After just one season at Georgia, Saban lured Smart to the NFL to coach safeties with the Miami Dolphins. During his first eight years as a coach, Smart only stayed at one place as long as two years.

But when Saban quit the Dolphins to take the Alabama head coaching job, Smart followed. This time he'd be in one spot for a while and wait for the right opportunity to emerge before becoming a head coach. Smart spent his first season in Tuscaloosa, Alabama, as a defensive backs coach. Promoted to defensive coordinator one year later, Smart quickly became known as a great defensive mind in the SEC and as one of the elite recruiters nationally.

At Alabama, Smart built some of the best defenses in a near decade span. In 2008 Alabama posted the third best total defense in the nation, allowing just 263.5 yards per game. That trend continued, and from 2009 through 2015, Alabama only fell outside of the top five in total defense once, which was in 2015. In that span, the Crimson Tide won four national championships with Smart coaching NFL talent such as Rolando McClain, Kareem Jackson, Marcell Dareus, Dont'a Hightower, Courtney Upshaw, Dre Kirkpatrick, Nico Johnson, Dee Milliner, Ha Ha Clinton-Dix, C.J. Mosley, and Landon Collins.

That kind of track record was yet another attractive quality for those at Georgia, starving for the kind of success Alabama has been able to accumulate over such a span. "It was critical to identify a person who would focus on a specific, defined process of developing championship football teams on and off the playing field," athletic director Greg McGarity said. "Someone who understands the true meaning of a student-athlete by actually experiencing it himself, someone who competed at the highest levels on the playing field, was mentored

Georgia athletic director Greg McGarity (right) introduces head coach Kirby Smart during a press conference on December 7, 2015. (AP Images)

by some of the very best in the game, and understood the specific ingredients necessary to excel at the highest levels of college athletics—Kirby Smart fits that profile. I believe Kirby Smart is the perfect fit for the University of Georgia."

When Smart was introduced, the emotion was apparent on his face. He stood at a podium in front of a crowded room at the Georgia Center for Continuing Education, the university's hotel and conference center, and choked back a couple of tears. The moment of taking over the Georgia program was one of immense enormity to a man who loved every moment of his playing days with the university. With

A Smart Player

Kirby Smart may not have been the most physically gifted football player to ever suit up at Georgia. But what those who played with him often say is that Smart was never going to be outsmarted or out-prepared on the football field. So the fact that Smart was a four-year letterman was no real surprise to anyone. A hard-nosed tackler with good football instincts as a safety, Smart was able to post 13 career interceptions with 11 of those coming over his final two years.

The most memorable game Smart appeared in was the 1997 contest against Florida, which Georgia entered as 20-point underdogs. The Bulldogs, thanks to a big performance from Smart and others, ended up flipping the script and defeated the archrival Gators 37–17. Smart had a huge game by picking off two passes and recording four tackles. "Nobody expected or gave us a chance in that game," Smart said.

Georgia occupying a special place in his heart, Smart long awaited the chance to coach there.

Georgia never really considered anyone else. Although McGarity and the university hired a search firm, Smart was the lone choice from the start. Names such as Tom Herman and Dan Mullen were thrown out there but were mostly considered backup options. Smart was the man Georgia zeroed in on from Day One.

And Smart patiently waited for an opportunity like Georgia. He didn't take a stepping-stone job. He'd been successful at Alabama and once received advice from Saban, his mentor, to take a major step up when the time came to leave. When Georgia came calling, of course, Smart was more than willing to listen. When the two sides came to an agreement, it was a perfect match for all parties involved.

While Smart was introduced as Georgia's head coach on December 7, 2015, he juggled being both Georgia's head coach and Alabama's defensive coordinator while preparing for a national championship for the latter. And Smart delivered for his former school one last time, helping Alabama win its fourth championship under Saban's leadership with College Football Playoff wins against Michigan State and Clemson.

It was evident he learned more than enough at Alabama, which is why he felt ready to jump into the limelight of being a major program head coach at a school like Georgia. "A lot of people have said 'Why not take a smaller school head job?'" Smart said. "I honestly feel my growth was better being in a large program, being around Coach Saban and learning how to manage a lot of the tough situations you deal with in the media. So for me, the most difficult thing for me is the timing of this and trying to move forward and grow and get the recruiting going."

What to Do and See

Visit the Arch

Oh, the Arch. It's the piece of architecture dear to the heart of every Georgia student—football fan or not. But that Arch contains a lot of history. As Athens, and the university, has changed over the many years, that arch has been witness to it all.

The Arch is located on Broad Street and represents the three pillars of the Georgia state seal—wisdom, justice, and moderation, which also represents the state motto. The Arch is considered the entry point into the University of Georgia's campus, where downtown Athens turns into a place of higher learning.

The Arch has become such a symbol of the university that it just might be the most photographed landmark on campus. There is also quite the superstition that accompanies the arch. Each freshman who arrives to Georgia is told he or she shouldn't walk underneath the arch until graduation. If a student chooses otherwise, they could risk being able to graduate. This belief apparently goes back to the early 1900s, when student Daniel Huntley Redfearn made a vow not to walk under the arch until he graduated. That story has been repeated since by professors and students alike.

The Arch was commissioned in 1856 and finished between then and 1858, but the exact date of completion is unknown. The exact date when the Arch went up on campus is also unknown. It was initially part of a fence to secure the campus when it was closed. The first known photograph of the Arch didn't appear until 1875. Over time the Arch became a meeting point on campus for students for a variety of reasons. It can be a place for students to celebrate, mourn, or protest. One of the worst moments in the Arch's history came in 1961, when students convened to show disapproval of the arrival of Hamilton Holmes and Charlayne Hunter-Gault, the first two African American students at the University of Georgia.

The Arch became a place for political protests, which continues today. Students gathered to protest the 1970 Kent State shootings, the

The First Public University

It's kind of like the chicken and egg question. Does the presence of a charter mean a particular institution is the first to offer higher education on a public scale? To those who love and support Georgia, this is the oldest state institution in the country. The charter granted by the general assembly was the nation's first in 1785. Abraham Baldwin then became the university's first president in 1786.

But Georgia didn't officially open its doors until 1801 and graduated its first class in 1804. Now, the competition: the University of North Carolina didn't have a charter granted until 1789—four years after Georgia's. But North Carolina was able to construct its campus and open doors for classes first in 1795, graduating its first class in 1798.

So there's the debate. Which state university was first, Georgia or North Carolina? You decide.

Persian Gulf War, and the Iraq War. It was also a place where a vigil took place following the devastation of the terror attacks on 9/11.

The Arch is quite possibly the most iconic structure on the campus at Georgia. It's practically synonymous with the university and a place where a great deal of history continues to exist and take place.

See the Dawg Walk

Georgia football games are an all-day affair. So whether kickoff is at noon, 3:30, or 8:00 PM, fans will be on campus many hours prior to partake in the varying traditions that exist.

A lot of that is tailgating and mingling with friends. But another special tradition fans gravitate to is the Dawg Walk, which takes place approximately two hours prior to every home game. Fans line up outside of the Tate Center, the location of a campus bus drop-off. The players then get off and greet thousands of fans to loud applause. The UGA Redcoat Band plays some music to accompany the players, as

Quarterback Jacob Eason greets a young fan during the Dawg Walk prior to the 2016 game against rival Georgia Tech. (AP Images)

they begin their walk inside Sanford Stadium. It's an exceptional event for families to partake in, especially those with smaller children.

The Dawg Walk was initially instituted when Vince Dooley became the program's head coach. When Ray Goff took over the program, he moved the Dawg Walk to the location it's at today before discontinuing it. Mark Richt brought the Dawg Walk back to life when he took the team over in 2001.

Those who attended the Dawg Walk in 2016 may have noticed a major difference in the players' appearance. From 2001 to 2015, Georgia players wore their jerseys when getting off the bus to walk into Sanford Stadium. A lot of this had to do with showing their names and numbers so fans could recognize who each player was.

When Kirby Smart became the team's head coach, he made one change to the Dawg Walk. Instead of jerseys the players now wear suits when entering the stadium. Smart decided to make this change because he wanted the Dawg Walk to have a more businesslike approach for his players. No matter what the players are wearing, the Dawg Walk continues to excite the fanbase when it's time for the Bulldogs to get to work on Saturdays.

Tailgate on Saturdays

The game itself is obviously the most important event on Saturdays. The activities that precede it come a close second. Tailgating is a rite of passage, or an art, for Georgia fans. Even for noon kickoffs, you can count on the Georgia faithful showing up in full force to bring plenty of food and drink their favorite beverages. There are quite a few spots for fans to tailgate. Some are, obviously, more family-friendly than others. But here's a rundown of the five top spots to set up a tailgate for a football Saturday in Athens.

The top spot would have to be the Tate Student Center Parking Lot. Given the popularity of this location, you will need to get there early and will more than likely need to acquire or purchase a pass to do so. But this is the place where the Georgia football team begins its Dawg Walk, which makes it a great place to eat, drink, and support the football team. It's a great place for children to come along as well, considering they'll get an up-close view at their favorite players as they step off of the campus bus to walk toward one of the many entrances of Sanford Stadium.

Another tailgating hot spot is the Legion Field parking lot, which is located close to the Tate Student Center parking lot. This is also a pass-only lot for those to tailgate at. But if you can get one of those, you're in for a good time. The parking lot is a great place to set up the tailgate since it's in walking distance to where the Dawg Walk begins. This is another family-friendly area kids are sure to love as well. This lot is sandwiched in between where the football team arrives, and possibly some form of entertainment will be on display as Legion Field often-times hosts a band or a performer.

If you don't need to be at the Dawg Walk, perhaps Clark Howell Hall is the location for you. Located nearby, but a six-minute walk to Sanford Stadium, this place offers the best of both worlds. The location is great, but you get to see the rest of campus come and go from your vantage point. This is a popular spot for tailgates as well.

The next two tailgate locations feature a younger crowd and can get a little rowdy. So be cautious if you choose this route. But they can also be a great deal of fun if you're into that sort of thing. Myers Quad is a beautiful green space located in between Myers Hall, Rutherford Hall, Mary Lyndon Hall, and Soule Hall. It's a very popular spot for tail-gates, especially for college students.

The fifth spot on this list is the most beautiful location but has under-gone some restrictions in recent years. North Campus has long been a popular spot to tailgate, thanks to its scenery, feel, and proximity to downtown Athens. And due to this, you're more likely to party harder here than any other place on campus. UGA officials noticed this, and the trash left behind, and set some rules for tailgating here, includ-ing the prohibition of kegs, amplified music, televisions, grills, and household furniture. If you're looking for a party and don't need the aforementioned items, North Campus is the place for you.

There are countless other places to tailgate in Athens, and there really isn't a bad spot. It's all about personal preference when selecting a spot to enjoy the pregame festivities before kickoff rolls around.

Catch the G-Day Game

College football seasons don't last long. Each team plays 12 games, and the lucky ones go on to play for a conference championship. From there only four go on to the College Football Playoff with the other postseason eligible teams playing in various bowl games. And then after that, it's over. From September through early January, it's a glorious time to be a college football fan. And then the waiting sets in as eight months must pass before the next season begins.

But there is one small reprieve for college football fans. That would be each team's spring game, and in Georgia's case, the G-Day Game. Admission is free, and everyone is welcome to attend. The game generally occurs in early to mid-April.

It's unknown how many G-Day spring games have been held in program history. But it's a chance for the teams to divide up and go against each other in front of the fans for the last time until the regular season kicks off. An older G-Day Game archived in *The Red & Black*, which is the student newspaper at the University of Georgia, was in 1967 when Vince Dooley was getting ready for his fourth season. That team would end the intrasquad exhibition in a 6–6 tie.

In 1989 former head coach Ray Goff switched the format up and had the current players scrimmage former players in a "return to glory" game. The present-day Bulldogs defeated the alumni 29–0, though it was a game players such as Buck Belue were able to participate in.

Another interesting moment in G-Day history came in 1996, when the Bulldogs were forced to host the annual spring game at Clarke Central High School. It was a sellout, considering the limited seating, and then-player and current head coach Kirby Smart intercepted two passes.

In recent history, only the 2000 G-Day game was canceled due to leaking pipes from under Sanford Stadium. Otherwise, this is an annual event for the fans.

For a while under former head coach Mark Richt, steaks were on the line in the G-Day game. Literally, steaks. The winning team used to be rewarded with steaks and lobster for winning. The losers got beanie weenies. Richt ended up scrapping that in 2012 when he found there were enough players who didn't mind eating beanie weenies in a losing effort. Under Richt, the most people he got to attend a G-Day Game came in 2015, when 46,815 people showed up at Sanford Stadium.

Kirby Smart, who replaced Richt, brought back the steak and beanie weanie tradition. At halftime of a Georgia basketball game against Arkansas in 2016, Smart asked for the fans to fill up Sanford Stadium for the G-Day Game. He asked for 93,000 fans to show up, which drew quite the applause. "I just want to tell everybody how great it is to be back home," Smart said. "I love the energy and passion here tonight. We want to see the same energy and passion at the spring game. We want to see 93,000 there to come out and support us."

It was quite the thing to say at the time. And although it was ambitious, there weren't many people who figured it would be done. Sure, there was a newfound excitement due to a new coach taking over the program. But 93,000 people for a spring game? Come on, now.

But the Georgia football social media team kept pushing it online, dubbing it #93KDay. And then the Bulldogs were able to book hip-hop recording artist Ludacris for a 15-minute pregame performance at

After a football victory, Georgia fans traditionally ring the Chapel Bell. (Jason Butt)

the last minute. When April 16, 2016, rolled around, it was a slow trickle of fans entering Sanford Stadium. And then by the end of Ludacris' short set, the fans had done it. Every seat in the stadium was filled, and some folks stood along the stairway to catch the first glimpse of the 2016 team.

The gesture by the fans brought plenty of emotion to Smart in his first year as Georgia's head coach. "For the fanbase to come out and support our program and support our kids the way they did, it touches me in my heart," Smart said. "It says that your fanbase has got your back and it's got your program's back. There were a lot of doubters out there that said it couldn't be done…But they came in droves, and I appreciate that, and our kids appreciate that."

Ring the Chapel Bell

Ringing the Chapel Bell is one of the oldest traditions Georgia holds. After a win students, alumni, and fans are free to ring the bell, which is located at the Chapel on North Campus, in celebration of a football victory. Anyone can do it, and often the sound of a ringing bell can be heard throughout the campus for hours when the Bulldogs win on Saturdays.

But how did this tradition start? This has been somewhat debated, though esteemed UGA athletics author and historian Patrick Garbin researched the first ever documented instance that the Chapel Bell was rung in celebration. In a somewhat surprising twist, the first documented ringing didn't occur after an on-campus game.

In 1894 Georgia defeated Auburn 10–8, and the Red and Black recorded a game-winning safety late in the game. The game was held at Athletic Park in Atlanta, so it wasn't played at Herty Field, which was located just yards from the Chapel Bell. But when news came back to Athens about Georgia's victory, the student body erupted in jubilation. According to an old *Athens Banner-Herald* story on the game: "[Students] were celebrating their football victory over Auburn in fine style. The chapel bell was ringing and the campus was ablaze."

As Garbin noted this doesn't mean this was the first time the Chapel Bell was rung following a Georgia football victory. It very well could have happened in the first ever game against Mercer in 1892. There just isn't any documented evidence of it occurring. So from a historical standpoint, the 1894 game against Auburn is the first recorded instance of fans ringing the Chapel Bell, which is now a major part of Georgia's tradition following wins.

When it became part of the football tradition, freshmen were required to keep ringing the Chapel Bell until midnight after home victories. If it was a victory against Georgia Tech, that bell would keep on ringing even after that. But now, there are no restrictions. If you're a 45-year-old alum back in town and caught a Georgia win, you can go up to the Chapel Bell and ring it pretty much any time of the day.

The Chapel Bell was constructed for $15,000 back in 1832. It actually replaced a previous bell that became too small for what the university wanted at the time. The bell originally had two purposes: to function with religious services and to signal when classes began and ended during a school day. The university doesn't need to use the Chapel Bell any more to signal when classes begin and end. But it's still a great piece of history put into use whenever Georgia wins a home game.

Wake Up with Jittery Joe's Coffee

Since 1994 Jittery Joe's has been an Athens institution. Originally located next to the old 40 Watt Club building, Jittery Joe's has long served the Athens area the best coffee in town. The variety of coffee is nearly endless as you can order a light roast to perk you up or a bold blend that will kick your energy level into high gear.

Once upon a time, the original downtown location was open 24 hours a day. The name Jittery Joe's actually comes from an episode of *The Simpsons*, with the creators parodying Thelma and Louise. The

Grabbing coffee at Jittery Joe's is the perfect way to start your Georgia gameday. (Jason Butt)

24-hour coffee shop Marge enters is called "Jittery Joe's." The founders searched for a trademark and didn't find one and thus created a physical Jittery Joe's location after the hit TV series.

Approaching three decades of business, Jittery Joe's now has nine locations in Athens. While the downtown location is open until 10:00 PM, the Five Points cafe is open until midnight. Given that Athens is a major college town, coffee is needed at all hours.

Jittery Joe's has expanded to four other cities in Georgia—Atlanta, Watkinsville, Macon, and Hoschton. Cleveland, Tennessee, also has a Jittery Joe's location. And believe it or not, there is an international location in Toyota Aichi, Japan.

Although Jittery Joe's has a house blend for those who want to buy a single cup of coffee, it sells various blends to buy for the home kitchen. One of the most popular would be the Morning Ride, a smooth, organic full-city roast that will wake you up on smell alone. The Travelin' Joe has a nutty finish that seems perfect for those on the go. The Terrapin Wake-N-Bake blend, in conjunction with the Athens brewery of the same name, has caramel undertones and a bold flavor that will easily get the heart pumping. The Terrapin Midnight Project is an espresso that was used in the brewery's 2009 stout. It can be bought as an espresso or coffee to enjoy.

Jittery Joe's roasts its coffee in small batches, which takes a bit more time than the major companies out there. The result is a splendid taste and an enjoyable jump-start to a new day. And on Saturdays, Jittery Joe's is the perfect way to begin the day before heading to Sanford Stadium to catch the Bulldogs between the hedges.

Become a Mama's Boy

Beware: if you want Mama's Boy, go early or late. If you hit it at peak hours, you will wait. That's because Mama's Boy is one of—if not *the*—premier places in town for breakfast and lunch—or brunch. Located at 197 Oak Street, there is a wait just about every day of the week during its peak rush hours. It's best to arrive to Mama's Boy between the hours of 7:00 and 8:00 AM. If it's a weekday, you'll avoid the rush after 1:00 PM. Even then, parking may be an issue due to how popular the place is.

Funny enough, the best time to eat there is during a Georgia game since just about everyone in town is at Sanford Stadium. But no one reading this book is heading to Athens to miss a football game, right?

There is a lot to like about the southern home-style cooking that Mama's Boy has to offer. The biscuits are flaky, soft, and perfect when you add the right amount of butter and raspberry jam. The biscuits are what Mama's Boy is known for and might not only be the best in the city, but also in the entire state. You can't go wrong with any of the breakfast entrees. The Mill Town Breakfast Plate features thick-cut bacon, two eggs, and cheese grits. The Pulled Pork Potato Hash & Salmon Cakes Benedict are also to die for.

As for lunch the Pimento Cheese Burger and the Pulled Pork Sandwich are great items to get. It's recommended, no matter what, to get a cup of coffee with your entrée. Jittery Joe's puts together a special blend for Mama's Boy, which is arguably its best-tasting coffee. A perfect diner-style coffee, you'll be asking your server for a refill more often than usual.

Enjoy some southern home-style cooking, soft biscuits, decadent cinnamon rolls, and other delicacies at Mama's Boy restaurant. (Jason Butt)

The most underrated item on the menu is the Cinnamon Bun. Make sure you have someone with you to share it. A large, decadent soft roll flavored with cinnamon and topped with gooey icing fills a standard-sized plate. There is a chance you thought you've eaten the best cinnamon roll on a previous day. You haven't—unless you've previously eaten the Mama's Boy cinnamon roll.

If you're in town for a football game, set the alarm clock early if you want to knock Mama's Boy off your bucket list. Get there at 7:00 AM and indulge in the best breakfast you've ever had.

Chow Down at The Varsity

"What'll ya have?"

That's the go-to phrase you'll hear when you step up to the counter to order something from The Varsity, a fast food joint that's been in Athens since 1932. It's long been a place to satisfy someone's cravings for a juicy cheeseburger or chili dog, as well as a sweet treat such as the famous Frosted Orange.

And okay, so the first Varsity was founded in Atlanta and originally called The Yellow Jacket. So what? The Varsity came to Athens and

You'll get tasty fast food and some unique slang when you order at the counter of The Varsity. (Jason Butt)

has been very much a gameday tradition for fans as the Atlanta location is for Georgia Tech supporters. Four years after the Atlanta location opened, Frank Gordy opened a location in downtown Athens at 101 College Avenue. In 1963, however, Gordy opened up a location on West Broad Street, which still stands today. The downtown Athens location closed 40 years after it opened.

The jargon at The Varsity is unique with the employees hollering out orders in a unique slang that caught on with customers years ago. Among other phrases, "Walk a Dog" is a hot dog to go, "Joe-ree" is coffee with cream, "All the Way" means with onions, and "Bag of Rags" means potato chips. The Varsity is a popular location before and after football games, but it's well worth the wait for a lot of people hungry for some of the most historic fast food the city of Athens has to offer.

Hit the Athens Bars on Friday Night

If you plan to make a long weekend out of a Georgia football game, be sure to get to Athens on Friday. That's when a lot of the fun in the fall happens.

It certainly helps that Athens offers a unique blend of activities for just about anyone of any interest. For the foodie, there are a lot of restaurants to dine at as a way to kick off a Friday night before a football game. But the top spot that's a must-stop is Last Resort Grill, and it's located on West Clayton Street in downtown Athens. In a city where restaurants seem to turn over as quick as football classes, Last Resort Grill has continued to thrive with its excellent southern style of food. As far as starters, the Fried Green Tomatoes are patron favorites. When it comes to main dishes, there's a whole lot of everything. The beef, pork chop, and fish dishes all come highly recommended as there really isn't a bad item on the menu. Then there are the decadent desserts. With the food being this excellent and the atmosphere of the former music club being as eclectic as it is, it's better to start your Friday night early at Last Resort Grill because this place will fill up and offer a long wait otherwise. It's an institution that will forever live on in Athens.

For those into music, Athens is a great place to catch a band on a Friday night. The historic Georgia Theatre, which was renovated and re-opened in 2011 after a devastating fire, has attracted a ton of well-known music acts over the years. If you get lucky, perhaps Drivin' N Cryin', Widespread Panic, Jason Isbell, or the Drive-By Truckers will get a date at the Georgia Theatre the day before a Georgia football game. In addition to the Georgia Theatre, the 40 Watt Club is another historic venue that hosts some quality bands. Located on

Renovated and re-opened in 2011 after a fire, the historic Georgia Theatre is a great place to catch a well-known musical act. (Jason Butt)

West Washington Street, the intimate setting always provides for a great show. Bands such as R.E.M., the B-52s, and Pylon got their start at the original 40 Watt Club prior to the move to West Washington Street. Since then newer bands such as The Killers, The Whigs, and Of Montreal have performed at the 40 Watt Club to big crowds.

Then, of course, you have the bar scene in Athens. The University of Georgia gets pegged as one of the nation's top party schools for a reason. Every street in downtown Athens is littered with a bar of your choosing. The college crowd generally hangs out at the kind of bars that seem to shut down and re-open every four or five years. That element will seemingly never change about Athens.

But the best Athens bars know how to get a consistent crowd, no matter the kind of trends that come and go. Allgood Lounge is seemingly a place that always stays crowded on game weekends, whether the Georgia football team is good that particular season or not. A lot of it has to do with the well-trained bar staff that can quickly take orders and return with drinks. It also has to do with the space the bar offers. It's a two-floor location with three bars—one on each story and one on the outside balcony. The list of beer and liquor is tremendous, and it has just about anything for anyone. And the crowd ranges from late college to late 30s. There are no frills with this place. It's a bar with just about everything for everyone.

Other locales to visit include Trappeze Pub, Wonderbar, and The World Famous. Trappeze Pub is a spot that offers some good food as well as a great cocktail menu. The beer selection is vast as well. Wonderbar will satisfy the inner old-school gamer in you, considering this is an arcade bar that features games such as Mortal Kombat and Ms. Pac-Man for patrons to play. You can also pull out games such as Connect Four to play if that's your thing. It's definitely a unique place with a lot of fun. The World Famous has some of the best wings you'll eat in downtown Athens. It's a different feel from a lot of the other bars in the area, and the whiskey cocktails are certainly worth trying.

Take a Picture with Uga

A bucket list item for just about every Georgia fan is to have his or her picture taken with Uga, the beloved bulldog mascot for the athletics program. The lovable and cute dog is at every game—home and away. The university ensures great care of the dog, preparing a room at the Georgia Center for Continuing Education, the on-campus conference center, just for Uga.

But as most people who have long followed the Georgia program know, the university didn't always use the bulldog as a mascot. The first animal brought to represent Georgia was for the second ever football game against Auburn on February 22, 1892, and it was a goat. Yes, Georgia student Bob Gantt brought his goat to the game, and historical accounts state that the goat wore a black shirt with the red letters "U.G." embroidered on each side. The goat also sported ribbons down his horns. In an attempt to rile Georgia's fans up, Auburn fans chanted, "Shoot the billy goat!" during the game.

In those days the university's football team wasn't referred to by a type of mascot or anything similar. They were commonly called the Red and Black or simply the Varsity. Over time there were quite a few mascots that roamed—or sat—on the sidelines for the football games. In 1894, for instance, Georgia had a dog serve as a mascot. A white bull terrier by the name of Trilby, owned by Charles H. Black, filled this role. Before being the football team's mascot, Trilby was the mascot and campus pet of the Chi Phi fraternity. Although Georgia wasn't officially referred to as the Bulldogs then, some suggest that this might have been around the first time the name was thrown around.

According to an Atlanta newspaper, per the Georgia sports communications staff:

"[E]very day Trilby took herself down to old Herty Field with her master for football practice. She ran signals with the best of them and became an accustomed figure on the athletic field...One morning, Trilby failed to appear for her breakfast and after a frantic search she was finally discovered proudly washing the faces of her newborn family, 13 white puppies…Late one dusky fall afternoon, Trilby appeared for a grid workout and scampering after her came her 13 children, darting through players' legs, barking and pace. 'Well,' suggested one of the players, 'Trilby has brought us a name, Bulldogs.'…Every time a game was played on Herty Field, the boys would floss Trilby and her 13 offerings up with red and black ribbons, and so attired they have gone down in history as perhaps the first 'sponsors' in southern football."

With Trilby being revered, that opened the floodgates for others who wanted their dogs to serve as the team's mascot. From *The Atlanta Journal* in 1962: "After the reign of Trilby and her family, chaos developed in the mascot department at the university. Many games had several, depending on which alumnus got his dog to the game first."

Another piece of evidence showing the football program's attachment to being the Bulldogs is from a patch uncovered by Atlanta resident Maury Ingram, who was a graduate of Auburn. The patch depicted a bulldog eating an Auburn pennant, with the phrase "Eat 'Em Up" written over it. According to author and football historian Patrick Garbin, who has written numerous UGA books, this badge "dates from 1898 to 1900."

It has been reported that the 1901 game against Auburn is when Georgia began referring to itself as the Bulldogs. Later, photographer Frederick J. Ball claimed he was the first to incorporate the bulldog as Georgia's mascot in 1904. The first time any of the sports were recognized in print as the Bulldogs came in 1911, when a writer only known as "Brown" dubbed the baseball team the Georgia Bulldogs in *The Atlanta Constitution*. Writer Clark Howell Jr. later referred to the Georgia basketball team as the Bulldogs in 1913.

It wasn't until 1916 that *The Atlanta Constitution* first called the football team the Bulldogs. But, according to Garbin, around 1919 or 1920, the basketball team became known as the Wildcats, thanks to a young and scrappy group of players. This caused the football team to adopt the same name. But after the fifth game of the 1920 season, Morgan Blake, a writer for *The Journal*, wrote "there is a certain dignity about a bulldog, as well as ferocity, and the name is not as common as 'Wildcats' and 'Tigers.'" After this, Georgia, as an athletics program, decided to call itself the Bulldogs.

For years Georgia would invite fans to bring their dogs to serve as mascots. Eventually, a university veterinarian was picked to bring his bulldog named Mugs to games. Mugs became a hit with the Georgia fans, and the beginning of permanently having a bulldog on the sideline for games was born. In 1938 a bulldog named Count, who happened to be a descendant of Mugs, was officially named the team's mascot in an on-field ceremony.

From here until the Uga bloodline began, it's a bit murky. According to UGA, four bulldogs were considered official mascots. Garbin, through his own research, lists eight. Garbin's research indicates that following Count—Bozo, Baldy, Mr. Angel, Tuffy, Butch, Stinky, and Mike served as UGA football mascots. Prior to Uga the dogs the university recognizes are Trilby (1894), Mr. Angel (1944–46), Butch (1947–50), and Mike (1951–55).

Now, that the background is out of the way, here is where the fun starts. In 1956 a man by the name of Sonny Seiler, who was enrolled in Georgia's law school, received a gift in the form of a white English bulldog from Frank Heard, a friend of Seiler's wife, Cecelia. The bulldog was offered as a belated wedding gift to the couple. While Seiler was studying law at the time, he was also selling football tickets for the athletics department. Seiler once joked that, "I did more studying than selling because we didn't have a very good team back then."

When the Seilers picked up the bulldog that April, he hadn't filled out yet. He was tall, skinny, and his chest was fairly small. But by the fall, the bulldog matured and looked the part of the traditional white English bulldog. Cecelia Seiler then went to JCPenney and bought a size 12 child's red shirt, put elastic in the neck and sleeves, cut a "G" out of black felt, and sewed it on the front. Before the first home football game in 1956, Seiler took the bulldog, adorned in his new outfit, to his Sigma Chi fraternity house to show it off. "After a few iced teas," as Seiler jokingly said in a lecture at the Terry College of Business in 2009, the Seilers and his fraternity brothers decided to take the bulldog to the game, even though that was never the initial intention. With the bulldog in attendance, Georgia defeated Florida State 3–0 and was photographed for the Atlanta newspapers.

The bulldog received a ton of attention from the Georgia fans in the stands. Noticing this, Dan Magill, who was the Georgia sports information director at the time, told head coach Wally Butts that the Seilers had a bulldog who could make for a good mascot since Mike had died the previous year. Without knowing this at first, Seiler went to work one Tuesday at the ticket office and found a note from his boss stating, "Coach Butts wants to see you immediately in his office." Scared at first and not knowing if his job was at stake, Seiler went to visit Butts. That's when Butts asked if he could use Seiler's dog to be the program's mascot. When Seiler agreed, Butts replied, "Good, then have him at all the games." That ended the conversation then and there with the Seilers' dog becoming Georgia's mascot.

How did the bulldog earn the name Uga? Seiler had a classmate named Billy Young, who suggested the name one day while the two were having coffee soon after the Seilers received the bulldog. Young suggested naming the bulldog Uga, a play on the UGA initials that have come to represent the University of Georgia. Seiler recalled saying in response to Young, "Billy, that's about the smartest thing I've ever heard you say."

The first Uga's full name was Uga I: Hood's Ole Dan. Uga I, at least according to Magill, was the grandson of the mascot who served in Georgia's 9–0 Rose Bowl win against UCLA on January 1, 1943. Uga I served as the beloved mascot for 11 seasons. He became the mascot under Butts, stayed under head coach Johnny Griffith three years, and remained under head coach Vince Dooley, who took the Georgia job in 1964. But as with any dog, Uga I's health began to decline, and it was apparent the road trips from Savannah, where the Seilers lived, to Athens weren't going to work for Georgia's first mascot anymore. Seiler filled Dooley in on the news, and that it would be time for a new mascot to take over. Fortunately for everyone involved, the Seilers bred Uga I, who was the sire to a litter of puppies. The family chose one and became a two-dog family, along with two children, Swann and Charles, at the time.

Prior to the start of Georgia's homecoming game in 1966, the first Changing of the Dogs ceremony took place. Charles walked onto the field with Sonny, along with the two dogs. When it was announced over the loudspeakers that it was time for Uga I to retire, the old dog sat down right in front of the cheerleaders who were holding his leash. It was a fitting moment for the gracious first Uga, who'd capably served as the university's mascot for more than a decade. When Uga II was led to the center of the field, the Sanford Stadium fans erupted in the chant, "Damn good dog!"

When Uga I died in 1967, athletic director Joel Eaves suggested that he be buried at Sanford Stadium. A small funeral ceremony took place to honor Uga I. His final record as a mascot was 53–48–6.

Uga II came along and saw the Georgia team win at a higher clip than before with Dooley hitting his stride as the head coach. And the Seiler family had grown to four children after the births of Bess and Sara. The family would drive up in a red station wagon with the parents in the front, and the four kids were in the back with the bulldog behind them.

Uga II had a remarkable run from 1966 to 1972 as Georgia won two SEC titles and appeared in five bowl games. The program went 42–16–3 under Uga II's watch. But Uga II was diagnosed with leukemia. His death paved the way for Uga III to come along.

Uga III was born on October 9, 1972, and pressed into action as a one-year old pup. One change that occurred with Uga in the 1970s was that Nonie Sutton became the dog's seamstress. Sutton would make the dog's jersey for gamedays. In addition Uga III also had an issue where his eyes were too dry. The UGA vet school cut a piece of his saliva gland out and inserted it by his eyes, which solved the problem by keeping them wet. On the football field, Uga III was quite the success. Georgia won the 1976 SEC title while Uga III was Georgia's mascot. But in 1980 Uga III got to be an up-close witness to the biggest achievement in Georgia history. The Bulldogs went undefeated in the regular season, which included a thrilling win against Florida thanks to a 93-yard catch-and-run from receiver Lindsay Scott. With Charles Seiler holding his leash, Uga III can be seen in that corner of the end zone Scott ran into on that particular play. That 1980 season would be the last for Uga III. His retirement ceremony took place early in 1981 at the Savannah Golf Club. Uga III's health began to decline, and that was evidenced by the Seilers needing to use a golf cart for the 1981 Changing of the Dogs ceremony, which just so happened to be his 100th career game. Not too long after Uga IV took over, Uga III passed away, and his career record was 71–32–2.

Uga IV was able to put a lot on his resume. He was quite possibly the most active Georgia mascot in his day. For starters he went to consecutive Sugar Bowls, following the 1982 and 1983 seasons. He was invited to attend the 1982 Heisman Trophy ceremony in New York at the Downtown Athletic Club since running back Herschel Walker was a finalist who went on to win the award. To this day folks joke about how Uga IV was a bigger media draw than Walker was—since no live mascot had attended the Heisman ceremony before. And Walker facetiously said how embarrassed he was for wearing a loud red jacket while Uga IV wore a black bow tie over his game jersey. Uga IV also traveled with the Georgia basketball team to its lone Final Four appearance ever in Albuquerque, New Mexico, in 1983. Uga IV would see the rest of the Dooley years and be on site for the first year of the Ray Goff era. Uga IV retired in 1989. Dooley would coin Uga IV as "The Dog of the Decade," considering all of the accomplishments he was on hand to witness: two SEC championships, nine bowl teams, the Heisman Trophy banquet, and the NCAA Final Four. Since the 1990 basketball SEC championship team began its season when Uga IV was still on hand, he received credit for that season too. Uga IV died of kidney failure on February 26, 1990. His time as Georgia's mascot ended with a career record of 77–27–4.

It should be noted that there was a stretch where Uga IV needed a substitute due to a left hind knee injury sustained when jumping off of a hotel bed before a 1986 game against Vanderbilt. In came Otto, a bulldog in the Uga line who looked the part outside of a brown spot on his lower back. But Otto quickly became a fan favorite after jumping out to a 2–0 record as the mascot. Entering the next game, the fans began to chant, "2 and 0 with Otto." Otto would go on to finish 3–1 in his four-game stint as Georgia's substitute mascot. And while Dooley said he never chose a favorite Uga, he certainly has a favorite substitute. "I have always had a great affection for those who came off the bench and performed, and he did that and had a great time," Dooley said.

As is customary, when one Uga departs, another one comes in. But the dog who became Uga V wasn't the original choice from the Seilers. A dog they named Magillicuddy after Dan Magill was primed to be the next Uga. But then another all-white English puppy on the Uga line was born, and this particular pup was going to have a longer time to be Georgia's mascot thanks to when he was born. And he was actually born only a little over a week after Uga IV passed, on March 6, 1990. So the Seilers named him Magillicuddy II and got him ready to be the new mascot in no time. Uga V presided under two head coaches— Ray Goff and Jim Donnan—and compiled a 65–39–1 record. But the wins and losses didn't define Uga V's time at Georgia. Three particular moments did, however. The first was in 1996 when Georgia outdueled Auburn 56–49 in a four-overtime classic. But the spectacular finish of that game was secondary to a moment Uga V had during it. Auburn receiver Robert Baker caught a pass and turned up toward the end zone to score. After notching the touchdown, Baker moved near Uga V, who was startled at the sudden movement. With Baker standing directly over the dog, Uga V responded by jumping high and attempting to bite him in his groin area. Uga V missed, of course, but a picture snapped by a *Montgomery Advertiser* photographer is part of Georgia lore. The picture has since been depicted in various works of art and is all around Athens. In the documentary *Damn Good Dog*, Charles Seiler, who was holding Uga V's leash during that moment, joked about the incident. "Had Uga landed where he intended to hit, it would have been a bad scene," he said.

In 1997 Sonny Seiler received a phone call from *Sports Illustrated* asking if it could send a photographer down to shoot Uga V for the magazine. *Sports Illustrated* was compiling lists of the best jock schools and the best mascots for the April 28, 1997 issue, and Uga V was to be a part of it. Little did Seiler know at the time that Uga V would be featured on the *Sports Illustrated* cover as the nation's No. 1 mascot. When the magazine hit newsstands, it was quite the surprise for those at Georgia.

But the feisty near-bite and magazine cover would pale in comparison to Uga V's other accomplishment during his tenure as Georgia's mascot. In the 1980s Seiler, as an attorney, represented Jim Williams, who was accused of the murder of Danny Hansford. This case went four trials and eventually resulted in an acquittal with Williams claiming self-defense. Author John Berendt became interested in the subject and the surrounding elements of the city of Savannah, Georgia, and wrote a book about the events titled *Midnight in the Garden of Good and Evil*. The book, released in 1994, became an instant success and was a 1995 finalist for a Pulitzer Prize for nonfiction. Seeing it fit for the storyline, Berendt wrote about Seiler and Uga IV in his book. Three years after the book's release, Clint Eastwood directed and produced a movie of the same name. And when casting the characters, Eastwood's team decided to bring Uga V on set to play Uga IV. Cecelia Seiler recalled an instance when Eastwood was petting Uga V, saying he'd make him a star. Apparently Eastwood wasn't too familiar with college football. "Clint, he already is a star," Cecelia said in response.

At the premier of the movie, Uga V got out of a limousine and sported a tuxedo.

Uga V may not have won an SEC championship during his time as the mascot. But Uga V marked the beginning of a mass marketing campaign as a symbol for the university. He retired in 1999 with a Changing of the Dogs ceremony. Only two months after his retirement, Uga V died on November 22, 1999. Uga V's funeral was open to the public based on how popular he'd become.

Uga V was replaced by Uga VI, a bowling ball of energy on the sideline, weighing in at a whopping 65 pounds. He could be rambunctious when needed. He was a charming pup who loved to interact and play with others. Taking over for Uga V in 1999, he finished the final two seasons of Jim Donnan's time in Athens and missed the Oahu Bowl since it would have been a long flight to Hawaii. But after Donnan left, Uga VI was along for the great turnaround of the Georgia football program when Mark Richt took over. Uga VI got to enjoy SEC championships in 2002 and 2005. He'd wind up becoming the winningest mascot in school history, witnessing 87 victories to 27 losses. But in June of 2008, Uga VI succumbed to congestive heart failure and died at almost 10 years old.

That brought upon his successor, Uga VII, who had a fine first season during Georgia's 10–3 campaign. But tragedy struck near the end of his second season, and Uga VII died unexpectedly due to heart-related causes on November 19, 2009. He was only four years old and ended his short-lived career 16–7. "We are all in a state of shock," Sonny Seiler said at the time. "We had no warning whatsoever."

When Uga VII passed, there wasn't a replacement ready to go. So Georgia went to the substitute well and picked out Russ to fill in. Russ was the half-brother of Uga VII and served as an interim mascot for the final two games of the 2009 season. Russ was then the mascot for the first six games of the 2010 season before Uga VIII, also known as Big Bad Bruce, was ready to go. But much like Uga VII, Uga VIII would have health problems as well. Following his introduction during a pregame ceremony before Georgia's homecoming game against Vanderbilt on October 16, 2010, Uga VIII would only be Georgia's mascot for six games. He was unable to accompany the team for the Liberty Bowl against Central Florida after being diagnosed with lymphoma. Uga VIII died on February 4, 2011 with only a 4–2 all-time record.

Uga VII and Uga VIII's deaths sent shockwaves through the Georgia community. And it left the Seilers scrambling for an Uga IX. In the meantime, the Seilers and Georgia turned back to the trusted Russ

Uga VII sits on the sideline during the fourth quarter of a 2008 game against Georgia Southern. (AP Images)

to take over the mascot duties once again. Russ kept his interim tag through the entire 2011 season and through the first two games of 2012. But even with some brown on his fur, which would deviate from the historical all-white coated Uga, a decision was then made to go with Russ as Uga IX. A ceremony indoctrinating Russ as Uga IX took place before Georgia's game against Florida Atlantic on September 15, 2012. And Uga IX was part of quite an astonishing season. The Bulldogs went 11–1 in the regular season and won the SEC East. They then played arguably the best game of the entire year against Alabama in the SEC championship but fell short 32–28. Uga IX would stay on through the 2014 season. In 2015 he retained the title, but it was obvious his age and health wouldn't allow him to be the team mascot anymore. So the Seilers turned to a young pup named Que to try the job out first before assuming the role in an official manner. It wasn't until late in the season, on November 21, 2015, that Que officially became Uga X. Uga IX came back for that game, a nighttime affair against Georgia Southern, for one last go-around in the spacious dog house afforded to him on the sideline. Used to the big home all year, Que was relegated to a much smaller crate for the game. Both Charles Seiler and his wife, Wendy Seiler, were on the field before the Georgia Southern game, allowing fans to take photos with both Uga IX and Uga X. It was a bittersweet moment for the family. "Russ is such a great dog, such a great mascot," Wendy said. "It's sort of sad to see him retire, but he's had a well-lived career as a mascot and he deserves a nice retirement. He was nice and ready go. He's full of energy. It's a big deal. It means a lot."

Uga IX died on December 21 at the age of 11, having gone out a winner with Georgia capturing an overtime victory against Georgia Southern. In his time as a substitute and official mascot, Uga IX compiled a 44–19 record. "Russ has endeared himself to the Georgia people over the last three years," athletic director Greg McGarity said after Uga IX's passing. "His dedication to duty when called upon has been exemplary, and it's fitting that he takes his place in the official line of Georgia mascots."

Que, now Uga X, is a spry young pup who finished his second season as Georgia's official mascot in 2016. The grandson of Uga IX, he handled the adjustment to gamedays well, Charles said, which made the choice fairly easy. When fans, photographers, reporters, cheerleaders, and anyone else with a field pass wants to take a picture with Uga X before a game, he's more than happy to oblige. It's one of the must-dos as a Georgia fan—to take a picture with arguably the biggest local celebrity, Uga, when he is in town.

When Uga isn't in Athens, he's in Savannah with the Seiler clan, though they're missing Cecelia, who passed away at the age of 80 on

Uga Burials

When Uga I died, then-athletic director Joel Eaves suggested he be buried in the confines of Sanford Stadium. That has been the custom since; each parting Uga was buried near the front of the south entrance to the stadium. Each dog is buried in a marble vault with an epitaph inscribed on his tomb. Flowers are placed on the graves before each home game.

Nine Ugas have been put to rest. Here are the epitaphs on each Uga's grave:

Uga I: Hood's Ole Dan—Damn Good Dog

Uga II: Ole Dan's Uga—Not Bad for a Dog

Uga III: Seiler's Uga Three—How 'Bout This Dawg

Uga IV: Seiler's Uga Four—The Dog of the Decade

Uga V: Uga IV's Magillicuddy II—Defender of His Turf

Uga VI: Uga V's Whatchagot Loran—A Big Dog for a Big Job, and He Handled It Well

Uga VII: Loran's Best—Gone Too Soon

Uga VIII: Big Bad Bruce—He Never Had A Chance

Uga IX: Russ—He endeared himself to the Georgia people. His dedication to duty when called upon was exemplary.

June 5, 2014. Although Sonny Seiler got the glory, Cecelia Seiler was the one often credited with taking care of the Ugas in the household. But she mostly did the behind-the-scenes work while Sonny acted as the "agent" for the celebrity dog.

For those who aren't involved with the Georgia athletics program, it may seem odd to place a bulldog on such a pedestal. To those at Georgia, there is nothing wrong with that. And as much as alumni and fans are proud of the dog, the Seilers are as proud to share their dogs with the University of Georgia.

The Players

Marvel at Herschel Walker

The freshman from Wrightsville, Georgia, took a handoff and cut to his left to hit the open hole. One player wearing orange stood in his way, and Herschel Walker needed to make a decision. Does he juke left or right or try another way to run around Tennessee safety Bill Bates? Or does he take a different path and just try to run straight through him?

Without much time to think, Walker acted on instinct. He went straight ahead, deciding to take Bates head-on. As he got close, Walker bent low to try and win the leverage battle. All Bates could do was try to hang on. Bates did his best to break down and wrap up, but Walker absolutely trucked Bates, knocking the future NFL safety on his back. Walker kept churning his legs and slipped through two other Tennessee defenders en route to the end zone for a touchdown. That score cut Tennessee's lead against Georgia to 15–9 with Walker scoring again a little later. In Walker's first game as a college football player, he scored two touchdowns and helped his team win 16–15. A star was born. "He's running all over people!" Georgia play-by-play announcer Larry Munson shouted on his call during the game. "Oh, you, Herschel Walker, my God Almighty, he ran right through two men. They had him dead away inside the nine. Herschel Walker went 16 yards. He drove right over orange shirts, just driving and running with those big thighs. My God, a freshman!"

The funny thing about it is that no one on Georgia's staff at the time was predicting Walker would be ready to take on such a big role so soon. Throughout Georgia's preseason practices, Walker wasn't doing anything out of the ordinary. It wasn't like he separated himself from the rest of the other Georgia backs. Georgia named Donnie McMickens the starting running back for the 1980 season because he'd earned it fair and square through camp. But after that first game from Walker? Yeah, things changed, and they changed fast. Walker quickly became the go-to running back out of Georgia's backfield and for good reason.

Walker grew up in Wrightsville, Georgia, a rural city that has a population of only 2,223 people. Starring for Johnson County High School, Walker terrorized opposing defenses for four years, totaling 6,137 yards and 86 touchdowns. He played linebacker as well and averaged double-digit tackles per game. He was also the Johnson County punter. He did all this and still managed to be his high school's valedictorian.

College football programs around the country were coming after Walker, hoping to gain his services. Georgia coaches made sure to be in his ear all the time, "bumping" into him at places they could legally do so under NCAA rules. Georgia head coach Vince Dooley figured it would be a tough recruitment to land him. But it wasn't that Georgia was competing with any other team. Georgia was competing with whether Walker wanted to continue playing football at the college level.

Walker's first choice was to join the Marines. Bullied as a child, Walker stored a lot of anger and thought the Marines would be a great place to channel it. What he may not have known at the time was that football served as his coping mechanism. When Walker was a middle schooler, he stuttered, was overweight, and was picked on by his classmates. The bullying hurt Walker time and again to the point where he'd do his best to avoid others. Then one day Walker went out to recess to join his classmates. That's when a kid beat up Walker in front of others. From that point on, Walker told himself that would never happen again. His focus went into overdrive. Walker began working out, which included doing push-ups and sit-ups in his downtime at home. All day, every day, Walker was working toward a goal of being the best at everything. He became the best athlete in Georgia, a unique blend of size, strength, and speed. He became a star student in the classroom. Walker wasn't going to be told he couldn't do anything anymore. The anger he had as a child was put to use in proving others wrong.

Fortunately for Georgia, Walker decided not to enlist in the Marines. He signed his National Letter of Intent with Georgia on April 6, 1980. But it wasn't until running over Bates that people realized he was the real deal and ready to play as a true freshman. That play, however, set the tone for the rest of his collegiate career. Walker's next game was against Texas A&M, which saw him run over a bunch of hapless defenders en route to 145 rushing yards and three touchdowns. The breakaway speed was unreal for someone his size—at 6'1" and 220 pounds, an imposing build for someone who was just 18 years old.

His first marquee showdown came against South Carolina with Walker going toe-to-toe with Gamecocks running back George Rogers, who had a fine game in his own right. But Walker zigzagged and bowled over the defense, toting the ball 43 times for 219 rushing yards. Although running over Bates might have been the most famous carry he had as a freshman, his best might have come against South Carolina. Walker took a handoff, found a crease, and hit his speed into turbo to the right sideline. Three South Carolina defenders came closing to make a tackle. And as they came closer, it looked like Walker would be tackled. But somehow, Walker sped past all three, hit his speed into an even higher gear, and sprinted down the sideline for a 76-yard touchdown. Rogers, a senior, would go on to win the Heisman Trophy that season, but it was evident who the best running back in college football was after that game. The monster games kept coming with Walker pummeling Florida on the ground for 238 yards on 37 carries in a 26–21 win. In the regular-season finale against Georgia Tech, Walker totaled 205 rushing yards on 25 carries in a win.

That set up No. 1 Georgia to play No. 7 Notre Dame in the Sugar Bowl. A win would give Georgia an undisputed national championship. But it appeared disaster was striking on Walker's second carry of the game. He was hit by a Notre Dame defender near the sideline and dislocated his shoulder. The training staff recommended Walker sit the rest of the way. Walker disagreed with that. He told them to put his shoulder back in place and to let him back in the game. The trainer obliged, and Walker continued to play. And he took a beating against

Notre Dame, which featured one of the best defenses in the nation. To that point, the Fighting Irish hadn't allowed one running back to run for 100 yards in a game. But for each hard hit he took, Walker delivered one right back at his opposition. Walker totaled 150 rushing yards and two touchdowns, all while managing the pain of a dislocated shoulder, in Georgia's 17–10 victory. The Bulldogs were named national champs, and Walker was the Sugar Bowl MVP. His first season concluded with an NCAA freshman rushing record of 1,616 yards to go with 15 touchdowns.

There was more of the same during his sophomore campaign as Walker carried Georgia on his back all season long once again. In Georgia's first two games against Tennessee and California, Walker ran for 328 yards. In a loss to eventual national champion Clemson, Walker ran for 111 yards. One of his best sophomore runs came against Mississippi, when he dove over a pile on a short-yardage run only to bounce off a couple of defenders, regain his footing, and run for a touchdown. Against the Rebels, Walker totaled 45 carries for 265 rushing yards. When Georgia faced Florida, the Gators jumped out to a 14–0 lead, and some of that had to do with a miscue Walker had on a kickoff return. But Walker more than made up for the early mistake by running the ball 47 times for 192 yards and scoring four total touchdowns. Two of those touchdowns were on runs, and the other two were receptions from Buck Belue. Walker ran for 165 yards against Auburn and for 225 yards against Georgia Tech. He couldn't be stopped at all.

The Bulldogs were then set to play Pittsburgh in the Sugar Bowl once again. In order to repeat as national champs, the second-ranked Georgia squad needed a win and a Clemson loss. But the Pittsburgh defense was a little stingier than what he'd faced earlier in the year. Walker still managed to total 84 rushing yards and 53 receiving yards with Georgia holding a late lead. But Pittsburgh quarterback Dan Marino found receiver John Brown over the deep middle for a 33-yard touchdown with only 35 seconds left to play. The Panthers defeated the Bulldogs 24–20. Walker's second season was even more impressive statistically than his first. He ran for 1,891 yards and 18 touchdowns. His yards per carry average went down, but that's just because Walker was taking more carries than he had previously. He essentially was Georgia's offense. Teams knew what was coming, and it didn't matter. Walker was a running back ahead of his time—given the style he played with at the size he possessed.

As a junior Walker seemed to run even harder and even faster. But in the first game of the season, Walker dealt with an injured thumb and was limited in his usage. The Bulldogs were still able to win that game

In his last regular-season game for Georgia, the marvelous Herschel Walker runs for a chunk of his 162 rushing yards against the Rambling Wreck. (AP Images)

against Clemson and avenge the previous season's loss. After a win against BYU, it seemed Walker was rounding back into form following the injury. In games against South Carolina, Mississippi State, and Mississippi, Walker combined for 507 rushing yards and five touchdowns. The stats kept piling up, and the wins kept coming. Georgia would end the regular season undefeated at 11–0 and earn another Sugar Bowl berth. This time it would be against Penn State in a true national championship game.

But before the Sugar Bowl, Walker was invited to the Downtown Athletic Club in New York for the Heisman Trophy presentation. Walker was easily the favorite to win the award and had a guest accompany him—Georgia's adored mascot, Uga IV. Walker won the Heisman decisively, earning 1,926 points. Stanford quarterback John Elway finished second with 1,231. Since stats in bowl games didn't count then, Walker entered the Sugar Bowl with a junior season of 1,752 yards and 16 touchdowns. That gave him an SEC record, which still stands today, of 5,259 career rushing yards. His 49 career rushing touchdowns are second all time in the SEC to former Florida quarterback Tim Tebow's 57.

Against Penn State in the Sugar Bowl, Walker ran for 102 yards and a touchdown, but that wouldn't be enough. Penn State defeated Georgia 27–23, giving the Nittany Lions the 1982 national championship. It was tough pill for Georgia to swallow, knowing how close it was to winning two titles in a three-year span.

Walker had originally planned to return for his senior season to try and help Georgia win another national championship and to pick up a second Heisman Trophy. At that time the NFL didn't allow for non-seniors to enter its draft. But the USFL had just formed, and it allowed for early entry. Without entering its draft, Walker signed a contract with the New Jersey Generals. After doing so, Walker expressed regret and hoped to return for a senior season instead. However, it was too late to do so. Walker's college eligibility was done, and he was now a professional.

If Walker would have been available at Georgia, the Bulldogs would have had an excellent chance to win a fourth SEC title and a second national championship in four years. Without Walker the Bulldogs still went 10–1–1 overall. Although there was a missed amateur opportunity, Walker signed a three-year contract with the Generals worth $5 million. He won the USFL rushing titles in 1983 and 1985. The league, however, folded after three years, which sent most of the best USFL players into the NFL. Walker signed with the Dallas Cowboys in 1986 but didn't run for over 1,000 yards until 1988, when he totaled 1,514 yards and five touchdowns. The surrounding talent, especially up front on the offensive line, did not do Walker any favors early on and caused NFL defenses to beat up on him. Five games into the 1989 season, Walker was traded to the Minnesota Vikings in a blockbuster deal that gave the Cowboys eight draft picks and helped build their early 1990s Super Bowl run. Walker would play 12 seasons in the NFL and still ranks 11th all time with 18,168 all-purpose yards. He retired from football after the 1997 season, his second year of a second stint back in Dallas.

Georgia never had a player like Walker before he arrived. It may never have another one like him ever again. Walker is regarded as one of the top college football players of all time. His three-year run at Georgia is unparalleled with the other greats of the game.

Learn About Georgia's First Heisman Winner

Frank Sinkwich didn't just draw attention to the University of Georgia football team when his college career began to take off as a sophomore. He brought more eyes to the southeastern brand of football, considering much of the attention was being paid to the northeast and midwest schools during those early years.

While Alabama, Georgia Tech, and LSU had some good teams that won national championships, the game was dominated by the other regions. Sinkwich, though, helped change the narrative with a versatile style of football in which he could do just about everything.

Sinkwich grew up in Youngstown, Ohio, after his birth in McKees Rock, Pennsylvania, on October 10, 1920. A son of Croatian immigrants, Sinkwich went on to excel in football at Chaney High School. He would go on to play for the Wally Butts-coached Georgia squad, leading the Georgia freshman team of 1939, known as the "Point-A-Minute Bullpups," to an undefeated season.

But it was in 1940 when Sinkwich began to shine as a Georgia football player. As a sophomore Sinkwich earned a spot on the All-Southern team thanks to big games in wins against Georgia Tech and Miami to conclude the season. In 1941 Sinkwich started emerging as a national name. In the third week of the season, Sinkwich broke his jaw. But surgeons wired his jaw shut and concocted a contraption to help protect his jaw during games. He also was fed an all-liquid diet of fruit juice, chicken broth, and baby foods that he'd ingest through a straw. The toughness exhibited rubbed off on his teammates throughout the entire season, considering his condition.

Sinkwich was nothing more than remarkable despite the injury. Against Florida, Sinkwich did everything possible to win the game for his team. He scored two touchdowns and then was called upon to attempt a field goal while holding only a six-point lead. Sinkwich made the 10-yard kick with the Bulldogs going on to win the game 19–3.

Sinkwich also had a dominating performance in that postseason's Orange Bowl against TCU. Sinkwich ran for 139 yards and completed 9 of 13 passes for 243 yards and three touchdowns in a 40–26 victory against the Horned Frogs. Before the bowl game, Sinkwich totaled a then-SEC-record 1,103 rushing yards, which stood for eight years. He was named an All-American for his spectacular season.

But it was his senior season when he went into college football lore forever. Sinkwich moved to fullback and shared the Georgia backfield with Charley Trippi. Sinkwich, though, still passed the ball quite frequently. He helped lead the Bulldogs to an 11–1 overall record, which included a 9–0 win in the Rose Bowl against UCLA.

Including the bowl game, Sinkwich ran for 828 yards and 17 touchdowns and passed for 1,456 yards and 10 touchdowns. A year after finishing fourth in the Heisman Trophy race, Sinkwich won the coveted award. He became the first SEC player to do so.

Sinkwich played in the NFL and was an All-Pro with the Detroit Lions from 1943 to 1944, but a knee injury cut his football career short in 1945. Sinkwich would remain involved in Georgia athletics and helped raise money for the construction of Butts-Mehre Heritage Hall, which acts as the office and training facility for the football program. He earned entry into the College Football Hall of Fame in 1954.

Sinkwich died on October 22, 1990, but has long been memorialized at Butts-Mehre Heritage Hall, where his retired jersey is on display. On the second floor of the building, his 1942 Heisman Trophy is also in the case, where it's displayed for all to see.

Remember Georgia's Most Athletic Star

Seven decades have passed since Charley Trippi last played a game for Georgia. And to this day many still hold on to the belief that there has never been a football player more athletic to suit up in the red and black than Trippi. Back in the leather helmet days, football players did a little bit of everything.

Trippi was a fine passer and a bruising runner. Born in Pittston, Pennsylvania, on December 14, 1920, Trippi excelled at both football and baseball. He accepted a scholarship to attend the University of Georgia and starred on the undefeated freshman team. He was then part of the 1942 team led by Frank Sinkwich, who won the SEC's first ever Heisman Trophy that season. But it was Trippi who stood out in that season's final game with 115 rushing yards in a 9–0 Rose Bowl

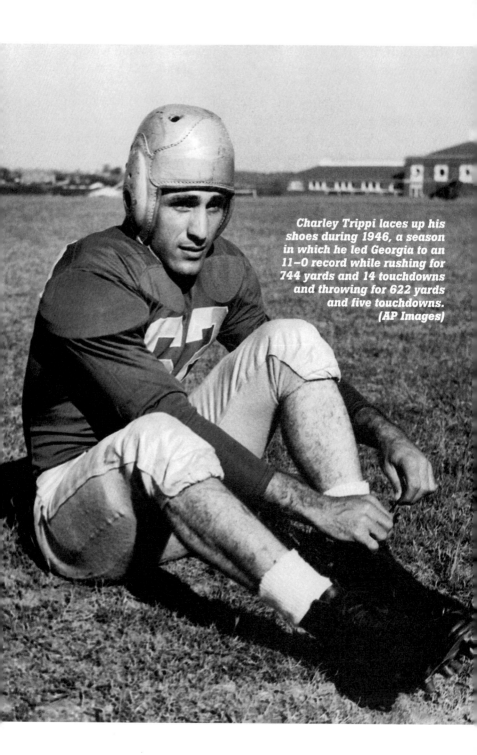

Charley Trippi laces up his shoes during 1946, a season in which he led Georgia to an 11–0 record while rushing for 744 yards and 14 touchdowns and throwing for 622 yards and five touchdowns. (AP Images)

win against UCLA. That game should have put Trippi on an immediate trajectory to college football superstardom. But those plans would be put on hold as he was asked to fight for his country in the United States Air Force. After running for 672 yards and eight touchdowns as a sophomore, Trippi missed the next two and a half football seasons to fight in World War II.

He returned to the gridiron midway through the 1945 season after his discharge and picked up where he left off. Trippi rumbled for 253 rushing yards and 10 touchdowns in only six games. And in the final game that year against Georgia Tech, Trippi was electric in a performance that saw him total 323 passing yards and 61 rushing yards. The passing number and the total yardage (384 yards) were SEC records at that point in time.

Trippi turned around and captained the 1946 team to an undefeated 11–0 record and an SEC championship. He ran for 744 yards and 14 touchdowns while throwing for 622 yards and five touchdowns. Trippi was certainly one of the most well-rounded football players to ever play for the Bulldogs.

But he wasn't just a football player. Trippi was an All-American baseball player in 1946 as well and played professionally for the Atlanta Crackers in 1947. Trippi would go on to have a lengthy NFL career of nine years with the Chicago Cardinals. And he was a hot commodity in those days, considering he could run, throw, catch, and kick the football.

Coming out of college, the All-America Football Conference's New York Yankees thought they were going to sign Trippi to their franchise. But the NFL's Chicago Cardinals ponied up $100,000 to sign Trippi instead. In those days $100,000 was an incredible sum of money, and that amount garnered headlines everywhere.

Trippi didn't disappoint in his professional career. In nine years with the Cardinals, Trippi ran for 3,506 yards and 23 touchdowns. He also caught 130 passes for 1,321 yards and 11 touchdowns during the duration of his professional career. As a punter Trippi averaged 40.3

yards per attempt. Trippi played some defense, too, recording four interceptions and an interception for a touchdown during his pro career.

Trippi earned entry into both the National College Football Hall of Fame (in 1959) and the Pro Football Hall of Fame (in 1968). During his enshrinement speech for the Pro Football Hall of Fame, Trippi made sure to thank Wally Butts, his coach at Georgia. "You know, football has enriched my life in so many ways that it also gave me a lifetime ambition and made me set many goals, but this goal today is probably the greatest," Trippi said. "When you play football, you have many great weekends, but this to me would be a lasting weekend I'll never forget. You know in football, when you have success a lot of times, it often reflects on the people that you played with and to them I want to say thank you. And in conclusion, I'd like to pay tribute to those people primarily responsible for my career. First my high school coach, Paul Shebby, then my college coach, Wallace Butts, and my pro coach, Jimmy Conzelman. I want to thank them for their guidance and their understanding."

Learn How Sapp Broke the Drought

Losing to Georgia Tech is painful. Every person who has ever cheered for Georgia understands this. Although the Yellow Jackets have had their shares of success, Georgia has dominated the series since the first game on November 4, 1893. So for the modern-day fan, imagine what it would be like to lose to Georgia Tech for eight consecutive seasons.

That's exactly what occurred from 1949 to 1956. The Yellow Jackets owned the rivalry from that span and went ahead in the all-time series 24–22–5 thanks to a 35–0 win in 1956. Georgia fans were sick over this and desperate for a turnaround against their hated rival. The 1950s, in general, were a tough time to be a Georgia fan. So after 364 days—from December 1, 1956 to November 30, 1957—Georgia had its chance to end the skid against Georgia Tech.

The game was in Atlanta and definitely one that would not be friendly to a passing game. The temperature dipped below 32 degrees with a wind blowing throughout. The Bulldogs were in the midst of another losing season so a win over Georgia Tech would be a mighty accomplishment as well as a saving grace.

Georgia and Georgia Tech put on a defensive slugfest, and through two quarters the game was knotted up at 0–0. The Yellow Jackets then had the ball in the third quarter and put the ball on the turf. None other than Theron Sapp, a native of Dublin, Georgia, recovered it for the Bulldogs. Sapp was also a ball carrier at fullback, so he came back on the field for the ensuing possession. Facing a third-and-long situation from the Georgia Tech 39-yard line, the Bulldogs hit a pass for 13 yards and a first down. From there Sapp took over. He powered his way on six consecutive carries down to the 1-yard line before being handed the ball again. On the seventh carry, Sapp bulldozed his way into the end zone for a 7–0 lead. That's all Georgia would need in this game as the Bulldogs snapped the eight-game losing streak.

Sapp was hailed as a hero instantaneously. The Georgia faithful had reason to celebrate, and Sapp was a major reason why. Sapp, who would go on to be a captain on the 1958 Georgia team, had his jersey retired only two months after the Bulldogs beat the Yellow Jackets for the second consecutive year to even up the all-time series. "I never dreamed my jersey would be retired," Sapp said.

That 1957 game is often referred to as why Sapp had his jersey— which hangs next to those belonging to Frank Sinkwich, Charlie Trippi, and Herschel Walker at Butts-Mehre Heritage Hall—retired so quickly. But that oftentimes overshadows the great career Sapp had at the University of Georgia. Sapp was All-SEC in 1957 and 1958 and was named Georgia's back of the decade from 1950 to 1959. Head coach Wally Butts once said Sapp was "the best offensive fullback I ever had."

As the story goes, Sapp almost wasn't able to play football at Georgia. A football injury in a high school All-Star Game caused three vertebrae to crack, and doctors advised him not to play the sport anymore. Butts said Sapp still had a scholarship offer, no matter what. Even Butts advised Sapp not to play the game for the sake of his health. But Sapp recovered during his freshman year and played on the B team as a sophomore. Then he made history as a junior and capped his career off as a captain. "Walker won the national championship for Georgia and was awarded the Heisman trophy, but to older Bulldogs who suffered through the 1950s, Sapp's breaking the drought was greater," former Georgia Tech head coach Bobby Dodd said. "He silenced eight years of bragging from Tech students and alumni. Breaking the drought was a remarkable achievement."

Groove to the Junkyard Dogs

The Dogs, they jump when they're mad
They're mighty, mighty tough, and man's that's bad
We're big, we're little
But yet, we'll tell our opponent they ain't seen nothing yet
Dooley's Junkyard Dogs
Dooley's Junkyard Dogs
They'll bark, they'll howl
Man, those Dogs are really, really proud
Dooley's Junkyard Dogs
Dooley's Junkyard Dogs

Those words were sung by none other than the Godfather of Soul himself, James Brown, a Georgia Bulldogs fan in his own right. Collaborating on the track, "Dooley's Junkyard Dogs," with "Happy" Howard Williamson, who wrote some words down after being inspired by Georgia's defense during a win. Williamson was with the Georgia Sports Radio Network at the time and got Brown and his band to record the song. Brown even performed the song at a couple of games, including one in 1977 against Kentucky at Sanford Stadium, in which Prince Charles of England came to visit.

The song was released in Atlanta with around 100,000 copies not too long before Georgia's annual meeting against Florida in 1975. The second time Brown performed the song at a UGA game was in fact before the annual rivalry game at the Gator Bowl. Notable in this is the fact the Junkyard Dogs moniker Brown sung about hadn't been tagged with the Georgia defense for very long either.

The season prior Georgia did not have a good performance on the defensive side of the ball. In the pre-spread offense era, the Bulldogs gave up 23.8 points and 356.5 yards per game during the 1974 season. Those numbers were the worst in Georgia history since the 1905 season and were deemed unacceptable by then-defensive coordinator Erk Russell. With only a couple of defensive starters returning for the 1975 campaign, Russell figured he'd need to tweak the scheme to suit its strengths. Gone was the 5-2-4 formation used previously. In was the split-60 defense, which saw the defensive ends outflanking the offensive tackles with the defensive tackles attacking the gaps in the middle.

In addition to the schematic change, Russell had an idea for an identity change. He decided to call his defensive group the "Junkyard Dogs." "There isn't anything meaner than a junkyard dog," Russell told the *Athens Banner-Herald* before the 1975 season. "They aren't good for nothing except for being mean and ornery. That's what we want our defense to be."

Russell also reportedly went to Roger Dancz, the director of Georgia's Redcoat Marching Band, and asked him to play Jim Croce's 1973 song, "Bad, Bad Leroy Brown" due to a lyric about a junkyard dog.

> *And it's bad, bad Leroy Brown*
> *The baddest man in the whole damned town*

Badder than old King Kong
And meaner than a junkyard dog

Croce in a 1973 interview explained why he included the term "junkyard dog" in his hit song. "Yeah, I spent about a year and a half driving those $29 cars, so I drove around a lot looking for a universal joint for a '57 Chevy panel truck or a transmission for a '51 Dodge," Croce said. "I got to know many junkyards well, and they all have those dogs in them. They all have either an axle tied around their necks or an old lawnmower to keep 'em at least slowed down a bit, so you have a decent chance of getting away from them."

Georgia's defense did a much better job during the 1975 season of keeping running backs and quarterbacks from getting away from them. The yards per game average dropped from 356.5 in 1974 to 307 in 1975. Georgia went 9–3, and the Junkyard Dogs nickname stuck from there on out. The Bulldogs would go on to win the SEC in 1976 and the national championship in 1980. Going forward, Georgia would be known as having a top-notch defense.

To this day the Georgia defense is referred to as the Junkyard Dogs when it plays

G.A.T.A.

Erk Russell was quite the motivator as a coach, whether it was as an assistant at Georgia or as the head coach of Georgia Southern, which was rebooting its football program. One of the terms Russell coined while he was at Georgia was the acronym G.A.T.A.

As legend has it, Russell saw a sweatshirt that read G.T.A.A., which stood for Georgia Tech Athletic Association. Russell then rearranged the letters to spell out G.A.T.A., which stood for "Get After Their Asses." It was a term the players loved and it stuck with the Georgia program for decades.

Under head coach Mark Richt, "G.A.T.A." was spelled out on the back of Georgia football shirts issued to players. Richt kept the acronym up throughout his 15-year tenure at Georgia, and it was on the walls and chalkboards throughout Butts-Mehre Heritage Hall. It's certainly a tradition Russell began at Georgia that will live on forever.

at a high level on Saturdays. And the Redcoat Band still plays "Bad, Bad Leroy Brown" during games thanks to the tradition Russell and Dancz started in 1975. "We got to be savages and junkyard dogs, just have a little mean streak in us," Georgia outside linebacker Davin Bellamy said. "It's just the intensity for the game. It's all for the fun of the game."

Take Pride in Running Back U

Georgia has earned the moniker Running Back U by quite a few pundits over the years for the rich tradition in producing players at the position. And it isn't solely due to the kind of seasons Herschel Walker put together while he was running between the hedges from 1980 through 1982. Georgia has established a rich history of running backs over the years, especially in the seasons since Walker's dominance.

But prior to Walker etching his name as one of the best to ever suit up in a college football uniform, there were quite a few great players to don the red and black in the backfield. Among those were Georgia legends Charley Trippi and Frank Sinkwich. Trippi played for Georgia in 1942, fought in World War II, and then rejoined the Bulldogs in 1945, which was highlighted with a 239-yard performance in a win against Florida. Sinkwich led the nation in rushing in 1941 with 1,103 yards and was Georgia's first Heisman Trophy winner in 1942 as both a runner and passer.

Just a couple of years before Walker came on the scene, Willie McClendon was running with a lot of power inside Sanford Stadium. Before Walker set the single-season rushing record, McClendon held it with 1,312 yards during the 1978 season.

Once Walker's time in Athens was over, Lars Tate showcased his ability in the mid-1980s by running for 3,017 yards and 36 touchdowns in his career. Tate still has the second-most carries by a Georgia running back in program history with 615. But it was in the 1990s when it seemed Georgia started to churn out quality running backs year after year.

Garrison Hearst displayed a blend of speed and power to the tune of 1,547 rushing yards in 1992, which placed him among the Heisman Trophy finalists that particular season. Hearst was a bell cow throughout his career, totaling 228 carries in 1992 while toting the ball 543 times in the three years he appeared in games.

Robert Edwards moved from cornerback to running back in 1995 and was electric from the start. Totaling five touchdowns (four rushing, one receiving) against South Carolina in the 1995 season opener, it sure seemed Edwards would be destined for big things at the position. But an injury-plagued career in Athens thwarted his potential. Even so, Edwards was still able to amass 2,033 rushing yards and 27 touchdowns in three seasons with 908 rushing yards and 12 touchdowns coming during his senior season. Edwards was drafted by the New England Patriots in the first round of the 1998 NFL Draft.

During the 2000s Georgia was able to get quality production from running backs like Verron Haynes (207 yards against Georgia Tech in 2001), Musa Smith (1,324 yards in 2002), Thomas Brown (875 yards in 2004), and Kregg Lumpkin (798 yards in 2006). But it was Knowshon Moreno who took the position at Georgia to another level.

During Moreno's two seasons, as a redshirt freshman in 2007 and third-year sophomore in 2008, he became only the second Georgia running back in program history to record multiple 1,000-yard seasons—1,334 yards and 14 touchdowns in 2007 and 1,400 yards and 16 touchdowns in 2008. Moreno's ability to juke defenders out of his shoes and tendency to spring back off of the ground after being tackled electrified the Sanford Stadium crowd each time he took the field. Moreno also had two incredible highlights in 2008. Against Central Michigan Moreno hurdled a defender in a blowout victory, which was captured and converted into photographic lore by those shooting the game. On the road at Arizona State, Moreno took a toss to his right

Georgia's all-time leading rusher with 5,259 yards, Herschel Walker poses with Uga IV and the dog's owner before winning the 1982 Heisman Trophy. (AP Images)

and leapt into the air from just inside the 5-yard line. As his body dove toward the end zone, he eventually landed across the goal line for a touchdown in one of the more athletic plays of the season.

In 2012 Georgia recruited Todd Gurley and Keith Marshall to campus, which turned into highlight play after highlight play. Gurley and Marshall would form the tandem "Gurshall"—a combo term that was also named after Herschel Walker and a moniker the two would come to dislike—and form quite the duo. As freshmen Gurley ran for 1,385 yards and 17 touchdowns, and Marshall ran for 759 yards

Georgia's Career Rushing Leaders

1. Herschel Walker (1980–82): 5,259
2. Nick Chubb (2014–17): 3,424*
3. Todd Gurley (2012–14): 3,285
4. Garrison Hearst (1990–92): 3,232
5. Lars Tate (1984–87): 3,017
6. Knowshon Moreno (2007–08): 2,734
7. Rodney Hampton (1987–89): 2,668
8. Thomas Brown (2004–07): 2,646
9. Kevin McLee (1975–77): 2,581
10. Sony Michel (2014–17); 2,411*
11. Frank Sinkwich (1940–42): 2,271
12. Willie McClendon (1976–78): 2,228
13. Musa Smith (2000–02): 2,202
14. Tim Worley (1985–86, 1988): 2,038
15. Robert Edwards (1995–97): 2,033

At the time of publication, Chubb and Michel were still in school competing in their senior seasons.

and eight touchdowns. Marshall would go on to deal with an injury-ridden career after his freshman season, and Gurley would deal with similar setbacks. As a sophomore Gurley dealt with injuries but still ran for 989 yards and 10 touchdowns. And as a junior, Gurley began the year as a Heisman Trophy candidate before a suspension for signing autographs for money took four games from his season. When he returned Gurley ran for 138 yards in a game against Auburn. But his college career came to an end that day as Gurley sustained a torn ACL in the fourth quarter. Gurley would go on to be drafted with the 10th overall pick by the St. Louis Rams, who have since moved to Los Angeles, in the 2015 NFL Draft.

But when Gurley was suspended and injured, another running back was able to step up and take center stage. Cedartown native Nick Chubb began the 2014 season fourth on the depth chart as a true freshman behind Gurley, Marshall, and fellow freshman Sony Michel. But with Marshall and Michel injured and Gurley suspended, Chubb was thrust into the spotlight in Georgia's 2014 game against Missouri.

As if he was picking up where the others left off, Chubb bulldozed through the Tigers en route to 143 yards and a touchdown on 38 carries. From there Chubb ended his freshman season with 1,547 yards and 14 touchdowns despite only starting eight games. Chubb became an instant star in Athens with high hopes for his sophomore season.

After running for 120 yards or more in each of Georgia's first five games of the 2015 season, Chubb took a carry to his left against Tennessee, took a hit and planted his left leg awkwardly on the Neyland Stadium turf. His knee bent the opposite way, which resulted in a torn PCL, MCL, and LCL. Chubb's season was suddenly done— with 747 yards and eight touchdowns attached to his name. The running back he came into Georgia with, Michel, took over lead running back duties and rushed for 1,161 yards and eight touchdowns in a lead role.

As juniors in 2016, and after former head coach Mark Richt was fired and replaced by Kirby Smart, the running game faltered due to some inconsistencies along the offensive line in a brand new offensive system. For the most part, Chubb and Michel stayed healthy and were able to end the year strong. Chubb finished with 1,130 yards and eight touchdowns with Michel totaling 840 yards and four touchdowns.

The conclusion of Chubb's junior year moved him into second place all time in rushing yards with 3,424. In doing so Chubb passed Gurley, who totaled 3,285 rushing yards during his three years in Athens. It was long assumed that Chubb would head to the NFL and end his running days at Georgia after his junior season. But in a surprise turn of events, Chubb elected to return for his senior season, which gives him an outside chance to surpass Walker's SEC record of 5,259 rushing yards. Chubb would need to run for 1,835 yards as a senior in 2017.

Michel, who totaled 2,411 rushing yards in his first three seasons, also elected to come back for his senior season. Georgia has continued the trend of recruiting stellar running backs to the program too, but Chubb and Michel didn't follow the trend some of Georgia's best backs have done when given the opportunity to turn pro after three years. Both decided to stick around with Georgia with hopes of achieving a championship. "It's tough because I could easily go to having a ton of money from where I am now," Chubb said. "But my whole mind-set is I'm just grateful for everything. I have a chance to come out here and play football at the University of Georgia another year, which is what kids dream of. I'm not just going to pass that up for selfish reasons. I'm grateful, I'm thankful."

Appreciate the Quarterback Legacy

Georgia has long been a destination for some of the best quarterbacks in the nation, going all the way back to the early 20th century. One of the early greats was George Cecil "Kid" Woodruff, of whom then-coach Alex Cunningham said, "I would rather see that little bunch of nerve leading my team than any man I have ever seen." Woodruff was Georgia's quarterback in 1907 and 1908 before taking the 1909 season off to travel. He returned a year later for two final seasons and became a captain in 1911.

Woodruff would later become Georgia's head coach from 1923 to 1927. David Paddock was also a leather-helmet era quarterback who rose to prominence at Georgia during his time from 1912 to 1915. Paddock, according to the university's sports information department, is the only player in program history to have the student body petition for his availability with the football team. Paddock, who grew up in Brooklyn, New York, would go on to become an All-American in 1914. He made the All-Southern team three times during his time at Georgia.

Buck Cheves earned the distinction of being the quarterback on Georgia's first team that called itself the Bulldogs. He also led what was called the "Ten Second Offense" and didn't wear a helmet during games. His on-field ability led *The Red & Black* student newspaper to pen this ode to him:

O! Cheves! O! Cheves!
In south, thou art rough,
The enemy grieves
When thou show'st thy stuff,
Thou art like a hurricane,
Thou hittest them hard,
God pity the man
Whom thou dost guard

Johnny Rauch was an excellent and well-known Georgia quarterbacks in the 1940s. Rauch was a four-year starter who earned the starting quarterback job as a true freshman in 1945, which didn't happen again until 1991. Rauch's arrival marked a change in head coach Wally Butts' offensive philosophy, in which Butts decided to implement an offense in which the quarterback was the team's primary passer. Rauch would become one of the greatest quarterbacks in Georgia program history and posted a career record of 36–8–1. He became the first player in college football history to start four bowl games and passed for a then-NCAA best 4,044 career yards. As a senior in 1948, Rauch was named an All-American and the SEC Player of the Year.

But what was exceptional about Rauch's college career was that he didn't come to Georgia as a hyped recruit. Butts discovered Rauch, a Pennsylvania native, playing in a flag football game and invited him to join the team. From there, the rest is history. Rauch became the first quarterback in program history to throw four touchdowns in a single game, which occurred against Clemson. This feat didn't occur again from a Georgia quarterback until the 1993 season. Rauch would go on to be the second overall pick in the 1949 NFL draft. He was selected by the Detroit Lions but traded to the New York Bulldogs for a certain running back named Doak Walker. After three seasons in the NFL with the New York Bulldogs (renamed the Yanks in 1950) and the Philadelphia Eagles, Rauch embarked on a coaching career, which included stops at Florida, Tulane, Georgia, and Army in the college ranks. He'd spend the majority of the 1960s and 1970s as an NFL coach, which included being the head coach for the Oakland Raiders and Buffalo Bills.

Zeke Bratkowski became the UGA quarterback in the 1950s, as the team continued to throw the ball all over the field in Butts' prolific offense. Back in those days, throwing for 1,000 yards in a season was a big deal, and Bratkowski did in each of the three seasons—1951, 1952, 1953—that he started. Bratkowski totaled a then-SEC record 4,863 yards in those three years. But with all of that throwing came a ton of mistakes, especially in those early days when the passing game wasn't as refined as it is today. Bratkowski still holds an SEC record for 29 interceptions thrown during the 1951 season. While Bratkowski threw eight interceptions against Georgia Tech in 1951, he doesn't hold the SEC record as Florida's John Reaves threw nine in a game during the 1969 season, which is also an NCAA record. Bratkowski also threw 16 interceptions in 1952 and 23 interceptions in 1953. Even with all the picks, Bratkowski's yardage total was an NCAA best until 1961. He ranks seventh in Georgia history in passing yards.

After a stellar season on Georgia's freshman team in 1957, Fran Tarkenton took the reins as a sophomore in 1958 and became a nationally known name for his ability to direct an offense. After leading the Bulldogs to an SEC title in 1958, Butts opened up the offense for Tarkenton a year later. Tarkenton threw for 736 yards and six touchdowns as a junior and completed a then-SEC record of 60.8 percent of his passes. Tarkenton's greatest play came on November 14, 1959, when he faked to his right before throwing a touchdown pass to Bill Herron to defeat Auburn. The win gave Georgia the SEC championship. Tarkenton captained the 1960 team and was chosen as an All-American following his senior season. He had his best statistical season with 1,189 passing yards and seven touchdowns to go with 12 interceptions. After college Tarkenton embarked on an 18-year NFL career that included two stints with the Minnesota Vikings and the New York Giants. As a pro Tarkenton threw for 47,003 career yards and 342 touchdowns. Butts lauded Tarkenton as one of the best players he ever coached. "Tarkenton has no superior as a field general and ball handler," Butts said.

Following Tarkenton, Georgia had some pretty good quarterbacks take the field. Kirby Moore, Mike Cavan, Ray Goff, and John Lastinger all won SEC championships. Buck Belue was the quarterback on Georgia's 1980 national championship team, which of course featured all-world running back Herschel Walker. But in 1991 along came true freshman Eric Zeier, who would turn Georgia's passing records upside down. He became the first true freshman quarterback to start a game for Georgia since Rauch in 1945. He didn't start the season opener but ultimately replaced Greg Talley as the starter for the final six games of the 1991 season. He finished the year with 1,984 yards (a school record) and seven touchdowns and earned the SEC's Freshman of the Year award. This was only the beginning. As a sophomore Zeier threw for 2,248 yards, breaking his own record, and 12 touchdowns. This also marked the first time the UGA quarterback threw for more than 2,000 yards in a season. As a junior in 1993, it was an aerial assault for Zeier. On October 9, 1993, Zeier went off for 544 passing yards, which still stands as an SEC single-game record. In that game Zeier threw touchdown passes of 38 and 60 yards to Brice Hunter, a 51-yard bomb to Hason Graham, and a 10-yard strike to Terrell Davis. Zeier concluded the season with 3,525 yards, 24 touchdowns, and seven interceptions. Zeier had a stellar senior campaign as well, throwing for 3,396 yards, 24 touchdowns, and 14 interceptions. His college career concluded with a then-SEC best 11,153 yards and 67 touchdowns. Zeier's career passing yards record wouldn't stand too long as Tennessee's Peyton Manning moved into the top spot just three years later in 1997 with 11,201.

The 1990s also saw the arrival of Quincy Carter, who in 1998 became Georgia's first true freshman to start a season opener since Rauch. However, Carter had the advantage of being 21 years old as he played professional baseball out of high school before returning to college football. Carter's arrival to Georgia is of note because he signed a National Letter of Intent to Georgia Tech before playing pro baseball. When he decided to play college football again, he was able to get out of his contract and attend Georgia on scholarship instead. Carter ended his three-year career at Georgia with 6,447 yards, 35 touchdowns, and 25 interceptions before declaring for the NFL draft.

Up to this point, Georgia had plenty of quarterback history. And then the Mark Richt era began in 2001. From there, Georgia became a quarterback factory, putting out some of the better signal callers in the SEC. First up was David Greene, who redshirted in 2000 under Jim Donnan. After sitting out his first year on campus, Greene displaced Cory Phillips as the starter after the first game of the 2001 season, proceeding to become a four-year starter. Greene would then go down as one of the greatest passers in program history. As a sophomore Greene had one of the more memorable seasons anyone ever saw in Athens. His game-winning drive against Tennessee, which was capped with a touchdown pass to Verron Haynes for the win, went into Georgia lore instantly. Later that season Greene threw what would be a game-winning pass to Michael Johnson to beat Auburn. The Bulldogs faced fourth and 15 at the Auburn 19-yard line, and Greene lofted a pretty pass over the Auburn secondary and into Johnson's arms in the end zone, which stunned the Jordan-Hare Stadium crowd. His sophomore season concluded with 2,924 yards and 22 touchdowns. Greene would lead Georgia to an SEC championship and a Sugar Bowl win against Florida State. Greene's junior season saw an uptick in yards with 3,307 yards.

As a senior Greene split time with heralded recruit D.J. Shockley, who'd been waiting in the wings after redshirting his freshman season in 2001. But Greene was still the primary quarterback and threw for 2,508 yards and 20 touchdowns. One of Greene's highlights in 2004 was returning from a fractured thumb sustained early in the regular-season finale against Georgia Tech. The Bulldogs led 16–0 with Shockley playing in relief for Greene, but things began to turn in Georgia Tech's favor in the second half with 13 unanswered points. So Greene decided he needed to deal with the pain and re-enter the game. "I felt the momentum slipping," Greene said. "I took my coat off. I took the brace off my thumb. If anything, I just wanted to give us a little spark."

Greene could only take snaps out of the shotgun to ease the pain. He didn't attempt any deep throws, but he did complete a couple of passes on the fourth-quarter drive. It helped set up a 44-yard field goal from Brandon Coutu, which gave Georgia a 19–13 cushion that would wind up being the final score. Greene's career would come to a close after a win against Wisconsin in the Outback Bowl, which saw him throw for 264 yards, two touchdowns, and two interceptions. At the time Greene's career concluded with an SEC-best 11,528 yards, a mark that would stand for nine years.

With Greene having graduated, it set up one final season for Shockley, the No. 1 quarterback recruit in the nation coming out of high school in 2001. Shockley was the first to commit to Richt once he took the Georgia job but did think of transferring when it was apparent he would have to wait a while to play with Greene in control for four years. Shockley ended up making the most of his opportunity as Georgia's starting quarterback when he was a fifth-year senior in 2005. Shockley's season got off to a hot start against Boise State as he tossed five touchdowns in a blowout win. Shockley then led the Bulldogs to a 7–0 start before an injury kept him out of the Florida game. Georgia lost 14–10 without him. A week later Auburn upset Georgia on a late touchdown with Shockley throwing for 304 yards and two touchdowns in the game. Shockley's Bulldogs then reeled off three wins in a row to win the 2005 SEC championship. Shockley's final season saw him throw for 2,588 yards, 24 touchdowns, and five interceptions.

When Shockley graduated, Joe Terishinski III was initially tabbed as his replacement. But everyone inside and outside of Athens knew it was only a matter of time before a young freshman named Matthew Stafford would win the job and claim it as his own. It wouldn't be easy in his first season on campus. Tereshinski began the year as Georgia's starter, and Stafford served as his backup. But an injury to Tereshinski forced Stafford into action in the third week of the season against UAB. A not-so-hot start forced a temporary back-and-forth between him and Joe Cox for the quarterback spot for a few weeks, which included Cox's fourth-quarter comeback win against Colorado.

Tereshinski would return in losses to Tennessee and Vanderbilt, which forced Richt to go with Stafford for the remainder of the season. Although his first-season stat line—1,749 yards, seven touchdowns, 13 interceptions—wasn't the greatest, the light seemed to turn on in a win over No. 5 Auburn. Stafford went for 219 yards and a touchdown and also rushed for 83 yards and a score. It was the first big moment of Stafford's career, which was a launching pad for his next two years at Georgia.

Though that first year was a struggle, there was never much doubt that Stafford would put together some fine performances on the football field. As former teammate and close friend Kris Durham once said, Stafford could barely relax while watching a football game on television when the two met on an official visit. "He could sit there when we were seniors in high school and he would read the defense and tell us what he would check to on certain plays," Durham told me in 2008. "You can even see it now. We'll be watching another college game, and he'll look at what the defense is and say, 'Okay, I would check to this play or this play.' He can't even sit back, watch, and enjoy a game. He just sits there and thinks the whole time."

Stafford, who came to Georgia with one of the strongest arms in the history of the program, led the Bulldogs to seven consecutive wins to close out the 2007 regular season, including a whopping 41–10 win against Hawaii in the Sugar Bowl. Stafford's statistical output was much better as he threw for 2,523 yards, 19 touchdowns, and 10 interceptions. As a junior Stafford was part of a team that began the year as the preseason No. 1 squad in America. Although injuries took a toll on the three-loss team, Stafford didn't disappoint at the position. The highlight of his junior year was a 42–38 road win against Kentucky, in which Stafford completed 17 of 27 passes for 376 yards and three touchdowns. Stafford threw the game-winning score to A.J. Green from 11 yards out with only 1:54 left to play in the game. Stafford would declare for the NFL draft and become the No. 1 overall pick by the Detroit Lions. He's gone on to have a successful career and is one of only five passers in league history to throw for over 5,000 yards in a single season. He's in elite company as Dan Marino, Drew

Brees, Peyton Manning, and Tom Brady are the only others to do so.

As Stafford was leaving Georgia, another heralded five-star quarterback was coming in. His name was Aaron Murray, and he was a much different quarterback than Stafford. The future Lions star was the NFL prototype, standing at 6'3" and 220 pounds in college. Murray was a bit shorter—6'0" on a good day—and just over 200 pounds. The big-time recruit from Tampa, Florida, could flat out play, however, and only needed a redshirt season to learn the Georgia offense.

Georgia's Career Passing Leaders

1. Aaron Murray (2010–13): 13,166
2. David Greene (2001–04): 11,528
3. Eric Zeier (1991–94): 11,153
4. Matthew Stafford (2006–08): 7,731
5. Quincy Carter (1998–2000): 6,447
6. Mike Bobo (1994–97): 6,334
7. Zeke Bratkowski (1951–53): 4,836
8. Johnny Rauch (1945–48): 4,044
9. Buck Belue (1978–81): 3,864
10. D.J. Shockley (2002–05): 3,555

As a redshirt freshman, Murray flourished statistically during a season that did not go according to plan. Although the Bulldogs finished with a 6–7 record and a loss to Central Florida in the Liberty Bowl, Murray's first year ended with an impressive stat line of 3,049 yards, 24 touchdowns, and eight interceptions.

After dropping the first two games of the 2011 season, Murray led the Bulldogs to 10 consecutive wins and an SEC East title. Along the way he threw for over 250 yards in games against Ole Miss, Vanderbilt, and Georgia Tech. The Bulldogs lost their final two games—in the SEC championship against LSU and in the Outback Bowl against Michigan State. But that sophomore season of 3,149 yards, 35 touchdowns, and 14 interceptions was enough to set up a memorable junior campaign. With Murray entering his third season, the Bulldogs received a lot of hype and were tabbed with a preseason No. 6 ranking in the nation. After four dominant wins, Murray and the offense were needed to hold off Tennessee in a 51–44 shootout. Georgia was riding high after a 5–0 start but ran into a hot South Carolina squad that pummeled the Bulldogs 35–7. Murray didn't have his best performance, but much of that had to do with an offensive line that couldn't withstand the pressure from a South Carolina front four that featured Jadeveon Clowney, who would go on to become the No. 1 overall pick in the 2014 NFL Draft. Murray was limited to 109 passing yards and an interception in the loss. Adding insult to injury, when Murray arrived back to Athens, he and roommate Christian Robinson, a linebacker for the Bulldogs, found their house egged and rolled with toilet paper. On top of that, Murray's parents had just informed him his father was recently diagnosed with cancer. "Probably the worst 12 hours of my life, but I know my family will push through," Murray wrote on his personal Twitter account soon after he was back from the South Carolina game.

Murray shook off the horrible news and put a lot of focus back on his team. Two weeks later and after a bye, Murray had one of the best outputs of his career. Against Kentucky he threw for 427 yards and four touchdowns in a closer-than-expected 29–24 win. Murray led the Bulldogs to wins in each of the remaining regular-season games en route to a second consecutive SEC East title. That set up a showdown with Alabama with a national championship berth on the line. Murray showed toughness, determination, and grit in the SEC title game. The game was one of the best of the 2012 season and came down to one final drive. Murray led the Bulldogs down to the 8-yard line with just a dozen seconds left to go.

Murray looked to the sideline, and the coaching staff signaled to run a play instead of spike it. The goal was to keep Alabama in a base defense and not let it adjust with the clock stopped. Murray took the snap with eight seconds to go and was looking for receiver Malcolm Mitchell on a back shoulder fade. But Alabama linebacker C.J. Mosley tipped the pass at the line of scrimmage. Chris Conley ran a short out route and turned his head as the ball fell in his direction. Instinctively, he caught the pass but slipped. He fell to the turf. Without any time-outs left, Georgia lost to Alabama 32–28 in an absolute heartbreaker.

Murray finished with 265 yards and a touchdown. "I can't sleep at night," Murray said a couple of weeks after the game. "I literally replay the entire game pretty much every night before I go to bed. It's stressful. It's a game that will probably haunt me the rest of my life, honestly."

Murray would return for his senior season in 2013. He put in a remarkable year, but it was cut short after an ACL tear sustained on Senior Night against Kentucky. Murray went down as arguably the greatest quarterback in program history, totaling SEC bests with 13,166 yards and 121 touchdowns.

Watch David Pollack, One of Georgia's Great Defenders

These days David Pollack may be more well-known as a TV star. Since joining ESPN in 2009, he has served as an analyst on *College GameDay,* the network's signature Saturday morning show. He also contributes to ESPN's daily college football news show *College Football Live* and several additional studio shows throughout the season. But before becoming a mainstay on ESPN, Pollack was one of college football's best defensive players.

Pollack didn't come to Georgia as a heralded recruit. He was a three-star project, according to some recruiting analysts, who was either going to play fullback or on the defensive line. No one knew exactly what Pollack would do when he got to Georgia. But head coach Mark Richt was confident that he could get a lot out of the local prospect from Shiloh High School, regardless if he was on offense or defense.

As a true freshman, Pollack proved the recruiting rankings weren't always right on. Pollack saw the field at defensive tackle and played in 10 games with four starts. Playing inside on the defensive line was where Pollack did most of his work in high school, and that's why he started off his career at Georgia along the interior.

But it was the offseason after the 2001 campaign that saw the beginning of a dominant defensive career for Pollack at Georgia. Richt and defensive coordinator Brian VanGorder decided to move Pollack to defensive end, a position he'd never played before. But Pollack's football IQ was high enough and he was such an athletic specimen that the Georgia coaches felt comfortable with the move. Pollack embraced it and quickly turned heads as a sophomore during the 2002 season, which became one of the best in Georgia history.

Look no further than Georgia's game against South Carolina. Both defenses came to play that day with Pollack ultimately becoming the difference in a Bulldogs win. About a minute into the fourth quarter and with Georgia leading 3–0, South Carolina possessed the ball deep in its own territory at the 6-yard line. South Carolina quarterback Corey Jenkins took the snap and rolled backward and to his right to buy some extra time. But there was Pollack, looking to make a key play in a big situation. Pollack faced a double team from the right tackle and the fullback. He shook off both blocks, and Jenkins continued to run outside on the designed play as opposed to staying in the pocket. By doing so it allowed Pollack to get to Jenkins quicker, and it looked like a sack or hurry was evident. Instead, Pollack went for the ball as Jenkins' arm came forward. With Jenkins about to release the ball, Pollack got his hand on it and knocked it down along Jenkins' back. Pollack's momentum carried him on top of the ball, which made him able to corral it for an interception and touchdown. It was one of the most remarkable plays of the entire 2002 season. "I could never do it again," Pollack said in an interview 11 years after the play. "It was a freak play that happens once, and you admit you can't duplicate it."

Georgia would win 13–7 thanks to Pollack's heroics. It would be the springboard for Pollack's exceptional career as one of the best—if not the best—defenders to ever suit up for Georgia. He'd go on to earn All-SEC first-team honors in 2002, 2003, and 2004, which included winning the SEC Player of the Year award as a sophomore and SEC

The 2004 SEC Defensive Player of the Year, defensive end David Pollack celebrates after recovering a fumble by Arkansas quarterback Matt Jones during the fourth quarter of Georgia's 20–14 victory. (AP Images)

Defensive Player of the Year award as a senior. As of 2017 Pollack is the only player to win the Ted Hendricks Award, which goes to the nation's best defensive end, twice (2003 and 2004). Pollack also won the Chuck Bednarik Award, the Lombardi Award, and the Lott Trophy in 2004.

Pollack's college career ended with 36 sacks, which ranks in the top 30 since that statistic was kept. Pollack continued his football career briefly in the NFL after he was selected by the Cincinnati Bengals with the 17th overall pick in the 2005 NFL Draft. He recorded 4.5 sacks as a rookie, which led to many thinking he'd have a breakout season in year two. But on September 17, 2006, against the Cleveland Browns, Pollack tackled running back Reuben Droughns and suffered a broken sixth cervical vertebrae. The injury ended his football career and led to him launching his broadcast career.

Pollack is one of many outstanding defenders Georgia has fielded over the years. In the same conversation as Pollack when it comes to his standing among the Bulldogs' elite would be Bill Stanfill. Born in Cairo, Georgia, on January 13, 1947, Stanfill would become one of the toughest and most determined defenders to ever play a down for the Bulldogs. The star defensive lineman was all business on the football field, someone who would lay crushing hit after crushing hit. A stellar three-sport athlete in high school, Stanfill would be the catalyst to Georgia's 1966 and 1968 SEC championship teams. A consensus All-American in 1968, Stanfill in that season also became the only Georgia player to ever win the Outland Trophy. "Bill was probably the greatest athlete as a lineman I ever coached," former Georgia football head coach Vince Dooley said. "He could have been a great tight end as well. Against the triple option, he was the only player that could take the quarterback, the dive back, and the pitch man. Bill was a great person, great warrior, and a great Bulldog."

Stanfill's exceptional collegiate career led him to be selected as the 11th overall pick by the Miami Dolphins in the 1969 NFL Draft. Stanfill recorded a sack in Super Bowl VII to help the Dolphins defeat the

Washington Redskins 14–7. Stanfill would be recognized for his great college career when it was all said and done. He was named to the UGA Circle of Honor, the College Football Hall of Fame, the 25-Year All-SEC Team from 1961–85, the All-SEC Quarter Century Team from 1950–74, and the 1960s All-SEC Team.

The Georgia football community mourned Stanfill's passing on November, 10, 2016 at the age of 69. He'll forever be remembered as the gritty and athletic defensive end who made a ton of plays for the team he loved so dearly. "On the field, he was a fierce competitor," former Dolphins head coach Don Shula said. "His toughness served as an example to the entire team and was a key reason why he was so respected by teammates and opponents alike."

Safety Jake Scott was a teammate of Stanfill's and was also a consensus All-American in 1968. His career was capped with a program record of 16 interceptions. Champ Bailey is one of Georgia's best defensive backs to ever play and was named an All-American in 1998. Bailey went on to have a Pro Bowl career with both the Washington Redskins and the Denver Broncos. Safety Terry Hoague recorded 12 interceptions during the 1982 season and finished fifth in the 1983 Heisman Trophy race. Defensive back Scott Woerner recorded 13 career interceptions and was inducted into the College Football Hall of Fame in 2016. Knox Culpepper had an incredible career, posting a single-game record 26 tackles against Georgia Tech in 1983. Vernon "Catfish" Smith is a name not many new-school Georgia fans may know, but he was on the All-Southern Conference team from 1929 through 1931. The greatness on defense continues with names like Boss Bailey, Thomas Davis, Richard "Le Sack" Tardits, Justin Houston, Freddie Gilbert, Richard Seymour, and Bill Krug. Leonard Floyd was an excellent pass rusher at Georgia and became the ninth overall draft pick by the Chicago Bears in 2016. The Bulldogs will continue this tradition for many years to come as they regularly produce talented defensive players.

GEORGIA DEFENSIVE CAREER LEADERS

TACKLES

1. Ben Zambiasi (1974–77): 467
2. Greg Bright (1994–97): 453
3. Tommy Thurson (1980–83): 448
4. John Brantley (1984–87): 415
5. Nate Taylor (1979–82): 390
6. Knox Culpepper (1981–84): 383
7. John Little (1983–86): 381
8. Randall Godfrey (1992–95): 365
9. Bill Goldberg (1986–89): 348
10. Amarlo Herrera (2011–14): 334
11. Tony Gilbert (1999–2002): 328
12. Jim Griffith (1974–77): 325
13. Mo Lewis (1987–90): 314
14. Orantes Grant (1996–99): 312
15. Terrie Webster (1985–88): 311
16. Corey Johnson (1993–96): 306

INTERCEPTIONS

1. Jake Scott (1967–68): 16

    Bacarri Rambo (2009–12): 16

3. Jeff Hipp (1979–80): 14

   Terry Hoage (1981–83): 14

5. Scott Woerner (1978–80): 13

   Jeff Sanchez (1982, 1984): 13

   Ben Smith (1987–89): 13

   Kirby Smart (1995–98): 13

SACKS

1. David Pollack (2001–04): 36

2. Richard Tardits (1985–88): 29

3. Jarvis Jones (2011–12): 28

   Jimmy Payne (1978–82): 28

5. Mitch Davis (1990–93): 27.5

6. Freddie Gilbert (1980–83): 26

7. Quentin Moses (2003–06): 25

8. Justin Houston (2008–10): 20

9. Josh Mallard (1998–2001): 18

10. Leonard Floyd (2013–15): 17

11. Greg Waters (1984–85): 16

12. Charles Grant (1999–2001): 15

13. Will Thompson (2001–02, 2004–05): 14.5

    Charles Johnson (2004–06): 14.5

15. Mo Lewis (1987–90): 14

16. Bill Krug (1975–77): 13

    Phillip Daniels (1992–95): 13

Listen to Larry Munson

L arry Munson didn't grow up a Georgia boy. During his youth he spent his time hundreds of miles away in Minnesota, the state where he was born. There was no connection to Georgia in the early period of his life, which might seem strange considering how embedded he was with the football and overall athletics program he would come to adore and love.

Munson was born on September 28, 1921, in Minneapolis and eventually graduated from the Moorehead State Teachers College in Moorehead, Minnesota. Using his discharge pay from the military following World War II, in which he served as a United States Army medic, Munson enrolled in a broadcast school. His first job after 10 weeks of training? A radio station role in Devil's Lake, North Dakota.

Munson did the small gig thing for quite a while before getting his first break in Cheyenne, Wyoming, of all places, as a play-by-play sports broadcaster, something he hadn't done before. "I was 20 years old and I read in a magazine want-ad somewhere that the University of Wyoming was looking for a play-by-play radio announcer to do its football and basketball games," Munson said. "I sent them a tape of me doing a play-by-play game. The tape was a fake. I went into the studio and taped me doing the play-by-play for the Ohio State-Minnesota game. I had never done sports or play-by-play before in my life. I recorded about seven or eight plays and added sound effects. I sent that in as my tape. Looking back on it now, I can really see just how bad that tape was. It was awful. When I got out to Wyoming, the guy I was replacing was named Curt Gowdy. Back then, I didn't know him from anybody. He was just another guy. He was led to take the job doing Oklahoma A&M football and basketball. I got the Wyoming job, and it paid $45 a week. Gowdy and I became good friends. His home was in Wyoming so we hunted and fished a lot together."

In Oklahoma City, Gowdy covered both Oklahoma and Oklahoma A&M before leaving to take a job covering the New York Yankees in 1949. From there, Gowdy recommended Munson for a job in Oklahoma City covering minor league baseball, and Munson followed his geographical path. Munson would eventually move to a city on his own. In 1952 he relocated to Nashville, Tennessee, and did numerous broadcasting jobs there. He called Vanderbilt football and basketball games. He hosted what some people believe was the first fishing show on television. Munson also worked as a disc jockey for a local radio station. In 1966 Munson landed a job covering the Atlanta Braves and called their inaugural season after the franchise moved down from Milwaukee.

But during spring training, Munson learned Ed Thilenius left his position as the play-by-play announcer for Georgia football games. He inquired about the job with Georgia athletic director Joel Eaves, whom he knew from his days covering Vanderbilt. Eaves offered the job during their first phone call, which became the beginning of a perfect partnership between Munson and the Bulldogs. "The Braves sent me to a car dealer to pick up a car to drive to their training camp in Florida," Munson said. "Before I left Atlanta, I picked up a copy of *The Journal*. When I got to West Palm Beach, I check into my room, threw the paper on the bed, hung up my clothes, took a shower, and lay down on the bed. Then I saw this box in the paper saying that Ed Thilenius was going to have to drop Georgia football. The next morning I called Joel Eaves at the university. He offered me the job that day."

Any time someone new steps in, a period of change and transition sets in. For Munson, a Minnesotan with no connections to Georgia, it might have taken some time. But by the 1973 season, Munson was hooked on the Bulldogs, and Georgia fans became hooked on him. One of his better-known calls from that season came in a win against Tennessee. Georgia won late on what seemed like an improbable play in which quarterback Andy Johnson ran for an 8-yard touchdown. "My God! Georgia beat Tennessee in Knoxville! Georgia has defeated Tennessee 35–31 in Neyland Stadium!" Munson exclaimed.

Much like all of Munson's great calls, the passion and exhilaration were on full display. The excitement he felt, like he'd been a lifelong Georgia fan, endeared himself to those who couldn't attend games and needed to listen to Munson call them on the radio. He served as the extension to the fanbase on gamedays, allowing the listener to feel the passion as if they, themselves, were sitting among the Georgia faithful at Sanford Stadium. No bias was hidden when he called a Georgia game. He became a fan, just like his listeners.

Over time, you could count on a great call from Munson in a tight game. There are so many to choose from. When Buck Belue pitched the ball to Anthony Arnold on a two-point conversion to defeat Georgia Tech in 1978, Munson yelled, "Arnold got it! Anthony Arnold got two points!" The Bulldogs defeated their rival 29–28. Earlier that season in a game against Kentucky, he delivered a Munsonism when placekicker Rex Robinson delivered the 29-yard game-winner against Kentucky, saying, "He kicked the whatchamacallit out of it!" When placekicker Kevin Butler booted a 60-yard game-winner against Clemson, Munson had the epic call, "Oh my God! The stadium is worse than bonkers! Eleven seconds! I can't believe what he did! This is ungodly!"

When Richard Appleby found Gene Washington, an aspiring track and field Olympian at the time, on an 80-yard touchdown pass off of a reverse in a 10–7 win against Florida in 1975, a year before the Olympic Games in Montreal, Munson said, "Washington caught it, thinking of Montreal and the Olympics, and ran out of his shoes right down the middle 80 yards! Gator Bowl rocking, stunned, the girders are bending now. Look at the score!"

Then, of course, there were two big calls in 1980. The first came against Tennessee in the season opener on the road. It didn't take long for a certain freshman running back by the name of Herschel Walker to establish his presence as one of the most dominant football players anyone has ever seen. Although there was plenty of hype surrounding Walker, Georgia's top commit in the 1980 recruiting class, no one had seen him in a football game yet. But on his first career touchdown run, a legend was made. And the legend was immortalized with one of the great calls of Munson's career. Walker bulldozed his way over Tennessee safety Bill Bates and rumbled his way in between two defenders for the score. Munson boomed his voice over the microphone in near disbelief at what he'd just seen out of the freshman from Wrightsville, Georgia. "He's running all over people! Oh, you, Herschel Walker, my God Almighty, he ran right through two men. They had him dead away inside the 9. Herschel Walker went 16 yards. He drove right over orange shirts, just driving and running with those big thighs. My God, a freshman!"

Later that season against Florida, and with the Gators believing they were close to wrapping up a win over the Bulldogs, Munson perhaps had one of the top two calls of his career. Undefeated and hoping to stay that way, the Bulldogs found themselves trailing late to their hated rival. It was third and 8 at the Georgia 7-yard line with only a minute to play in the game. The Bulldogs only had one timeout, and it sure seemed bleak at this stage of the game. But that's what miracles were made for and what Munson was made to record over the airwaves. Quarterback Buck Belue used a play fake before rolling right and away from the Florida pressure. He pointed down the field at receiver Lindsay Scott before launching the ball his way. Scott found an open spot against the Florida defense, caught the ball, and turned upfield toward the left sideline. Perhaps to his chagrin, there was nothing but open grass in that direction, and the track speed Scott possessed had him off to the races.

The legendary call Munson gave still gives Georgia fans goosebumps to this day.

"Florida in a stand-up five, they may or may not blitz, they won't," Munson began. "Buck back. Third down on the eight, in trouble, got a block behind him, going to throw on the run, complete to the 25, to the 30. Lindsay Scott, 35, 40. Lindsay Scott 45, 50, 45, 40. Run Lindsay! Twenty-five, 20, 15, 10, 5. Lindsay Scott! Lindsay Scott! Lindsay Scott!"

From here, the roaring Georgia fans at the Gator Bowl filled in for Munson for a brief moment in time. "Well, if you want a miracle we just got one," Munson said. "Incredible play, Lindsay Scott caught the ball around the 40. There were a couple of players who had an angle. He knew that he had to run as fast as he possibly could. Well, I can't believe it—92 yards and Lindsay really got in a footrace. I broke my chair, I came right through a chair, a metal steel chair with about a five inch cushion. I broke it. The booth came apart. The stadium, well the stadium fell down. Now they do have to renovate this thing. They'll have to rebuild it now. This is incredible. You know this game has always been called the World's Greatest Cocktail Party, do you know what's going to happen here tonight, and up at St. Simons and Jekyll Island, and all those places where all those Dog people have got these condominiums for four days? Man, is there going to be some property destroyed tonight! 26–21. Dogs on top. We were gone. I gave up, you did, too. We were out of it and gone. Miracle!"

That game kept Georgia's undefeated season and national championship hopes still alive. And the Bulldogs would take the momentum from that game and go into the 1981 Sugar Bowl to face Notre Dame for the national championship. Georgia would win and be crowned the 1980 national champions.

There were so many other famous calls Munson made. How about against Auburn in 1982 with the Tigers threatening late with a Sugar Bowl berth on the line? "Fourth and 17, I know I'm asking a lot, you guys, but hunker it down one more time!" Munson said. "Auburn up to the line on the 21…Dogs are in a 4, and [Randy] Campbell has a blitz on him."

Campbell's pass fell incomplete, which sent Munson into elation. "He threw a high, wobbly pass. They fight in the end zone, and the Dogs broke it up! They broke it up! They broke it! Ronnie Harrison, Jeff Sanchez got up in the air. We had pressure up the middle…The Dogs with 42 seconds…I won't ask you to do that again, you guys…Oh, look at the sugar falling out of the sky! Look at the sugar falling out of the sky!"

For Georgia fans, it didn't get much better than Munson. As cable television became prominent with ESPN securing football rights for SEC games, fans could watch their team play every Saturday instead of solely relying on the radio. But with Munson's ability to make the listeners feel as if they were there, many fans would mute the television and listen to the radio broadcast for the play-by-play and color commentary instead. Some fans attending the games would bring in headsets to try and get the game on the radio to hear Munson's calls.

Some believe the "Run, Lindsay, Run!" call is Munson's best. Others believe what he said at the end of Georgia's 2001 game against Tennessee was better. A lot of it may have to do with a generational gap, considering 21 years separated the calls. The latter also came in Mark Richt's first season against a Volunteers team ranked sixth in the nation. With the Bulldogs down 24–20, Georgia drove down to the Tennessee 6-yard line with only 10 seconds to go. Redshirt freshman quarterback David Greene took the snap and play-faked the ball to running back Jasper Sanks. Coming out of the backfield and left wide open and alone was fullback Verron Haynes, and Greene threw him a 6-yard touchdown.

Here's how Munson described the play: "Ten seconds, We're on their 6. Michael Johnson turned around, asked the bench something. And now Greene makes him line up on the right in the slot. We have three receivers. Tennessee playing what amounts to a 4-4. Fake, and there's somebody. Touchdown! My God, a touchdown! We threw it to Haynes. We just stuffed them with five seconds left! My God almighty, did you see what he did! David Greene just straightened up, and we snuck the fullback over! We just dumped it over. 26–24. We just stepped on their face with a hobnail boot and broke their nose. We just crushed their faces!"

As Munson would later recall, he didn't know what a hobnail boot actually was. He was in the euphoria of the moment and trying to make a call in reference to a jackboot worn back in World War II. But those who heard the call are glad he went with the hobnail boot instead.

Munson would continue calling every game until the 2007 season, when health reasons caused him to stop going to road games. On September 22, 2008, Munson suddenly retired. The September 6 game against Central Michigan, the second of that season, was his last. Munson said his health issues were preventing him from living up to the standards he was accustomed to as a broadcaster. "I can't express enough my deep feelings toward the Georgia football fans," Munson said in a release announcing his retirement at the time. "They have been so friendly especially during this most recent period of time. I feel I owe them so much more than I can give. I'll remember all the great times with the Dogs and have the fondest wishes and good luck toward them all."

Before Munson's retirement Scott Howard handled play-by-play duties with former UGA quarterback Eric Zeier doing the color commentary. This duo has continued calling home and away games since Munson retired.

Munson's health would decline even further over the subsequent years after his retirement. He died on November 20, 2011, a day after Georgia's 19–10 win against Kentucky.

"We are deeply indebted to Larry for his wonderful contributions to the University of Georgia," Georgia athletic director Greg McGarity said. "For over four decades, Larry poured his heart and soul into Georgia football. His passion, energy, and love for our Bulldogs were clearly evident at all times—especially on Saturdays during the fall. For those of us who were able to hear Larry paint the picture with his live play-by-play calls, we are very fortunate. For those who were able to know Larry, our lives were enriched by a once-in-a-lifetime treasure."

Munson died at the age of 89. Even though Munson is gone, he's still very much remembered by the Georgia faithful who lived through the calls he gave each Saturday. Munson's voice has been immortalized at Sanford Stadium through a voiceover played before kickoff of each game. As the Redcoat Band begins to play the Battle Hymn, the large-screen television looking over the West end zone displays a video commemorating the longtime Voice of the Bulldogs with these words:

> *Glory, glory to old Georgia!*
>
> *Heroes have graced the field before you: men with the hearts, bodies, and minds of which the entire Bulldog nation can be justifiably proud.*
>
> *The tradition of unbridled excellence demonstrated by these individuals and many others spans more than a full century.*
>
> *And now a new breed of Bulldog stands ready to take the field of battle to assume the reigns of their Georgia forbearers and continue that tradition, understanding that there is no tradition more worth of envy, no institution worthy of such loyalty, as the University of Georgia.*
>
> *As we prepare for another meeting between the hedges, let all the Bulldog faithful rally behind the men who now wear the red and black with two words—two simple words, which express the sentiments of the entire Bulldog nation: Go Dawgs!*

On the
Hardwood

Learn About Durham's Dogs

It had been a long, long time since Georgia's basketball program sustained consistent success over a period of time. You'd have to go all the way back to the 1920s and 1930s to find such a thing. Head coach H.J. Stegeman delivered 11 winning seasons in his 12 years as the head coach from 1919 to 1931, which is why Georgia's home court is called Stegeman Coliseum.

Rex Enright then inherited a team for the 1931–32 season that featured Vernon Smith, and the group went 19–7 and won the Southern Conference championship with a win against North Carolina in the finals. But by the time the 1940s rolled around, there weren't too many winning seasons to be had in Athens.

After six consecutive losing seasons from 1972 to 1978, the Bulldogs brought in Hugh Durham, who had been the head coach at Florida State for the previous 12 seasons. It was an interesting move for Durham to make at the time since he'd had success with the Seminoles—not to mention that's where he played basketball in college.

Durham's best season at Florida State came in 1971–72 when his squad advanced all the way to the NCAA championship, where it lost to UCLA 81–76. The Seminoles finished 28–5 that year and have yet to return to the Final Four since. Durham crafted a great legacy at Florida State, so it certainly made it exciting when he arrived in Athens for the 1978–79 season.

Durham had an immediate rebuild job to do and he got the Bulldogs to 14–14 in his first year and then 14–13 in year two. It was in 1980–81 when Durham began to get the Bulldogs headed in the right direction. Georgia opened that season with six consecutive wins before a 64–62 defeat to Florida State. From there Georgia experienced some ups and downs but was able to record a win against No. 3 LSU in the

SEC Tournament. The Bulldogs reached their first postseason tournament, the NIT, and advanced to the second round.

The following season Georgia was led by Dominique Wilkins, who put in highlight after highlight on the floor. Wilkins led the Bulldogs with 21.3 points per game as an unstoppable force. Although Georgia closed the season strong with wins against Auburn, Tennessee and Mississippi, an early SEC Tournament loss to Alabama was in store. Therefore, the Bulldogs ended up back in the NIT for the second consecutive season. This time, however, Georgia advanced all the way to the semifinals before losing to Purdue 61–60. It was a sign that progress was being made.

But after Wilkins' excellent season, he decided it was time for him to go pro and head to the NBA draft. Wilkins was taken third overall by the Utah Jazz but subsequently traded to the Atlanta Hawks months later due to Utah's own financial problems combined with Wilkins' preference not to play there. Without Wilkins, surely Georgia wouldn't be able to grow upon the NIT semifinal season?

Wrong.

The 1982–83 season saw Georgia reach heights it never had before—and never has since. Without Wilkins the Bulldogs needed others to help pick up the slack. Vern Fleming, Terry Fair, James Banks, Gerald Crosby, and Lamar Heard proved to be a formidable starting lineup and one that gave opponents fits. The Bulldogs jumped out to a 9–0 start, which included wins against Georgia Tech and Texas. Georgia proved to be the real deal when it recorded its first win against Kentucky since 1976. But over an eight-game span from February 5 to February 28, Georgia hit a skid and lost six of eight games. The Bulldogs were able to respond just in time en route to their first ever SEC Tournament title, defeating Alabama in the championship.

This set Georgia up for the NCAA Tournament, which saw it defeat VCU, St. John's, and a North Carolina team that featured none other than Michael Jordan. The win against the Tar Heels placed Georgia in its first and only Final Four. Durham's team would end its run there, losing to eventual national champion N.C. State.

The Bulldogs made it back to the NIT a year later in 1983–84 and then made an NCAA Tournament appearance once again in 1984–85. However, that NCAA Tournament appearance would later be vacated due to NCAA sanctions. The Bulldogs would go back to the NIT twice and the NCAA Tournament once over the next four years before putting together a great team in 1989–90. Georgia won the SEC regular season for the first time in school history with captains Alec Kessler and Mike Harron leading the way. Georgia lost, however, in the first round of the NCAA Tournament to Texas. A year later the Bulldogs would reach the NCAA Tournament again, marking the first time the Bulldogs went to the big dance in back-to-back seasons. Georgia was bounced in the first round in a tough overtime game against Pittsburgh.

The basketball team slid over the next four years, and Georgia reached the NIT twice. It's arguable that Durham was a victim of his own success. Four NCAA Tournament appearances in 17 seasons wouldn't be enough, as Durham was fired following the 1994–95 season. "I don't agree with the decision," Durham said in a news conference following his firing. "I just don't think it was justified. Our charge was to show significant improvement. It wouldn't be fair to our coaches or players not to say they did a very good job."

Vince Dooley, Georgia's legendary football coach who was the athletic director at the time, seemed to have wrestled with the decision to let Durham go. "This was an extremely difficult decision for me in light of my respect for and longtime friendship with Coach Durham," Dooley said. "I do, however, believe it is time to make a change in the direction of our basketball program."

Under Durham, Georgia basketball achieved heights it never had before. As of early 2017, Durham is still the only men's basketball coach to take two teams to their only Final Four appearance. After his time at Georgia came to an end, Durham sat out for two seasons

GEORGIA BASKETBALL'S CAREER LEADERS

POINTS

1. Literrial Green (1989–92): 2,111
2. Alec Kessler (1987–90): 1,788
3. Vern Fleming (1981–84): 1,777
4. Dominique Wilkins (1980–82): 1,688
5. Walter Daniles (1976–79): 1,679
6. Bob Lienhard (1968–70): 1,659
7. J.J. Frazier (2013–17): 1,628
8. Shandon Anderson (1993–96): 1,517
9. Terry Fair (1980–83): 1,492
10. Sundiata Gaines (2004–08): 1,469

REBOUNDS

1. Bob Lienhard (1968–70): 1,116
2. Terry Fair (1980–83): 923
3. Alec Kessler (1987–90): 893
4. Jerry Waller (1964–66): 867
5. Charles Claxton (1992–95): 840
6. Lavon Mercer (1977–80): 838
7. Chris Daniels (2000–04): 763
8. Carlos Strong (1993–96): 739
9. Tim Bassett (1972–73): 705
10. Trey Thompkins (2009–11): 693

ASSISTS

1. Rashad Wright (2000–04): 493
2. Sundiata Gaines (2004–08): 476
3. Litterial Green (1989–92): 446

4. G.G. Smith (1996–99): 440
5. J.J. Frazier (2013–17): 422
6. Vern Fleming (1981–84): 400
   Dustin Ware (2009–12): 400
   Charles Mann (2013–16): 400
9. Pertha Robinson (1993–96): 399
10. Rod Cole (1988–91): 379

BLOCKS

1. Lavon Mercer (1977–80): 302
2. Charles Claxton (1992–95): 247
3. Terrell Bell (1993–96): 168
4. Yante Maten (2014–): 149*
5. Dominique Wilkins (1980–82): 142
6. Donte Williams (2011–14): 136
7. Richard Corhen (1982–85): 125
8. Willie Anderson (1985–88): 122
9. Marcus Thornton (2011–15): 120
10. Chris Daniels (2001–04): 119

STEALS

1. Sundiata Gaines (2004–08): 259
2. Pat Hamilton (1985–89): 216
3. Shandon Anderson (1992–96): 212
4. Vern Fleming (1980–84): 205
5. Rod Cole (1987–91): 191
6. Levi Stukes (2003–07): 179
7. Ray Harrison (1995–99): 177
8. Rashad Wright (2000–04): 168
   Chris Daniels (2000–04): 168
10. J.J. Frazier (2013–17): 164

* At the time of publication, Maten was still in school competing in his senior season.

before returning to the coaching ranks to take over the program at Jacksonville. He concluded his career with 634 victories, which ranks in the top 30 all time. Durham was inducted into the College Basketball Hall of Fame in 2016. "When you've been in the profession as long as I have been and for someone to think I deserve this type of recognition makes you excited, but it also humbles you," Durham said. "After you get past that, you start thinking about all the people who enabled you to do this. I'm talking about the players, assistant coaches, and the administrators. At least for me, that's where most of my thoughts have been—all the relationships—because that's really why coaches have the opportunity to be considered successful."

Joining Durham in the 2016 College Basketball Hall of Fame class was his star pupil, Wilkins. As Wilkins went on to have the greatest success of any Georgia basketball player in program history, there has always been a fond memory of what Durham meant to him while at Georgia. "Hugh Durham is like a father to me to this day," Wilkins said. "He's a major part of my life, and a man I will always respect. To go into the College Basketball Hall of Fame with your coach is mind-blowing. I'm happy for him and also happy we will have an opportunity to reconnect and celebrate together."

Watch Clips of The Human Highlight Film

Dominique Wilkins has gone down as one of the best to ever lace his shoes up in the NBA. He's arguably the greatest dunker in the history of the entire sport. The hang time Wilkins exhibited on the many jams he threw down earned him one of the greatest nicknames of all time, "The Human Highlight Film."

On any given possession, Wilkins could spark a highlight type of play. And when Georgia was rebuilding its program shortly after Hugh

Durham assumed head coaching duties, Wilkins became an early catalyst to help shine some light on the basketball program.

Wilkins was born near Paris, France, on January 12, 1960, when his father was in the U.S. Air Force. Wilkins' family moved back to the United States and eventually settled in North Carolina during his high school years. Wilkins was a sought-after recruit by a lot of programs, considering the amount of highlight plays he was making in high school. He got to show off his game after being selected to play in the 1979 McDonald's All-American Game. He wound up choosing Georgia, becoming the key player Durham needed to bring attention and relevance to the basketball program.

Wilkins' impact was great from the start. As a true freshman during the 1979–80 season, Wilkins led the team in scoring with 18.6 points per game. With Durham donning the red blazer and Wilkins playing his style of basketball above the rim, it was a coach-player pairing made in heaven. A knee injury as a freshman would limit Wilkins to only 16 games played, but it was clear the Bulldogs had a special player on their hands.

The players who entered Georgia with Wilkins were pretty good too. Those players— Terry Fair, Derrick Floyd, and Lamar Heard—needed some time to gel with Wilkins. But Wilkins, who was appropriately nicknamed the Human Highlight Film, was a once-in-a-lifetime player. His fellow students at the time, who previously may have had no interest in Georgia basketball, were showing up for games just to see him put on a show.

Wilkins improved as a sophomore in 1980–81 by averaging 23.6 points per game. This time Wilkins was able to play in all 31 games, and the Bulldogs advanced to the NIT for the first time. This season also saw Wilkins score 32 points in a thrilling double-overtime loss to Kentucky, in which he scored in a variety of ways in front of a home crowd in Athens. Early on in the game, Wilkins recorded a blocked shot, scored a mid-range jumper, put in a breakaway layup, and hit a turnaround short-range basket off the glass.

As a junior in 1981–82, Wilkins averaged 21.3 points per game on Georgia's NIT semifinalist team. Wilkins decided to go pro after his junior season and even flirted with the idea after his sophomore year. Given his draft status at the time—validated by going No. 3 overall to the Utah Jazz and later traded to the Atlanta Hawks—it was the right move for Wilkins to make. But there will always be some wonder as to what could have been if Wilkins decided to stay for his senior season, considering the talented class of players with whom he came to Georgia. After all, that 1982–83 team put together the best season in Georgia history without Wilkins, going 24–10 overall and advancing to the Final Four.

But Wilkins was the most dominant player to ever come through Athens. In 1991 Wilkins had his No. 21 jersey retired by Georgia, making him the only player in the basketball team's long history to have this happen. Although Wilkins was inducted into the Naismith Memorial Basketball Hall of Fame for his vast accomplishments in the sport in 2006, he earned entry into the College Basketball Hall of Fame in 2016.

Known for his basketball career as a member of the Hawks, Wilkins was finally recognized for his accomplishments at the college level as well. "This is a huge honor for me and one that makes me feel cherished and honored," Wilkins said when his induction was announced. "I feel proud to have left a mark as a college player and am thrilled to be a part of this class. I truly appreciate the recognition as a basketball player and as a person."

Funny enough, Wilkins and Durham were inducted to the College Basketball Hall of Fame together. Durham still has fond memories of the Human Highlight Film's time playing for him in Athens. "It's meaningful because Dominique had so much to do with establishing Georgia Basketball," Durham said. "I'm really excited to have the opportunity to be inducted with him. I know we're all really excited about that. It's a well-deserved honor. I'm happy for Dominique and I'm happy for the University of Georgia."

Dominique Wilkins dunks over LSU during Georgia's 68–60 victory in the semifinals of the 1981 SEC Tournament. (AP Images)

Wilkins is easily the greatest ambassador for Georgia basketball. Before home games a hype video featuring Wilkins on the large-screen television asks fans to "Raise the Flag."

During a 2016–17 game against Vanderbilt, the Georgia marketing team held a promotion where they gave out Georgia No. 21 jerseys with Wilkins' name on the back to wear. And the reason Georgia is still able to use Wilkins' likeness to its advantage is because of the stellar professional career he had in the NBA.

Wilkins declared for the NBA draft in 1982 after his junior season. The move turned out to be a smart one because he was selected No. 3 overall by the Utah Jazz. The Jazz, however, traded Wilkins to the Atlanta Hawks a couple of months later for John Drew, Freeman Williams, and $1 million, making it easy for Wilkins' fans at Georgia to follow his career in Atlanta.

The 6'8" high-flying forward made the 1983 All-Rookie team and won the 1986 scoring title with an average of 30.3 points. Wilkins, who totaled 26,668 points in his NBA career, is one of only 20 players in NBA history to score 25,000 career points or more. Wilkins played in nine All-Star Games and won two NBA slam dunk contests. In 12 seasons with the Hawks, Wilkins averaged 26.4 points per game. Like Georgia, the Hawks also retired his No. 21 jersey.

But during his 12th season, the Hawks traded Wilkins to the Los Angeles Clippers, even though the Hawks were in first place in the Eastern Conference and Wilkins was their leading scorer. The Hawks would reach the East semifinals before bowing out to the Indiana Pacers.

Wilkins finished his professional career in stints with the San Antonio Spurs and Orlando Magic and also played overseas in Greece and Italy. Wilkins has since returned to the Hawks as a vice president and adviser. He also provides color commentary on Hawks games for radio broadcasts.

Appreciate Georgia's Final Four Appearance

I t's a big what-if for Georgia basketball: what would have happened if Dominique Wilkins stuck around for his senior season? The Bulldogs very well could have won the national championship, or at least that's what Wilkins told *The Atlanta Journal-Constitution* at his College Basketball Hall of Fame induction ceremony. "If I was there, we probably could have won the whole thing," Wilkins said.

But with those players who did return, that Georgia team was pretty darn good and came close to winning it all without Wilkins. Let's start with what occurred after the Bulldogs jumped out to a 15–3 start. All seemed to be going well at this stage of the season. The Bulldogs had defeated No. 10 Kentucky and were riding high.

But then came a major skid at a very inopportune time. First, the Bulldogs dropped a 70–59 decision to LSU at home. Two days later the Bulldogs lost by 15 points to Ole Miss. Two road losses later at Alabama and Mississippi State put Georgia on a four-game losing streak. Wins against Auburn and Florida helped, but then road losses to Kentucky and Vanderbilt made things look bleak for the Bulldogs, considering that meant they'd just lost six of their past eight games.

But basketball has a funny way of working out for teams with senior-laden talent, such as this particular Georgia group. Terry Fair, Lamar Heard, and Derrick Floyd were the veteran leaders, and Vern Fleming added 16.9 points per game, making for a formidable bunch. The Bulldogs rallied and closed with a win against Tennessee in the regular-season finale. But that only put them at 18–9 and tied for fourth in the SEC's standings with Vanderbilt, Tennessee, and Mississippi State. All four had gone 9–9 in conference play and 7–2 at home and 2–7 on the road. Georgia was very much on the bubble in the NCAA Tournament's then-field of 52.

But Georgia didn't tempt fate with the NCAA Selection Committee. It came together a week later after pulling off a 14-point win against Ole Miss, a team that defeated the Bulldogs by 15 just a little more than a month earlier. The Bulldogs then blew out Tennessee to advance to the SEC championship to face Alabama. In the SEC Tournament, Georgia caught a break when Kentucky lost early on. The Bulldogs, thanks to SEC Tournament MVP Fleming, went on to defeat the Crimson Tide 86–71 thanks to a hot shooting performance. Automatically, the Bulldogs were in the big dance.

By winning the SEC Tournament, Georgia earned a No. 4 seed in the subsequent NCAA Tournament's East region. Receiving a bye in the first round, the Bulldogs drew No. 5 seed VCU in the second round after the Rams defeated 12-seeded LaSalle in their opening game. Georgia survived a tough 56–54 win against VCU to advance to the regional semifinals. In this round the Bulldogs got No. 1 seed St. John's, a team that many figured could challenge for the national championship prior to the tournament's start. St. John's was led by Chris Mullen, who would go down as one of the best shooters in the history of basketball. Mullen averaged 19.1 points per game but wasn't the only one who put the basketball through the hoop often for the Redmen. David Russell averaged 15.4 points, and Billy Goodwin averaged 14 points per game, giving St. John's other options to turn to on the basketball court.

St. John's led the Bulldogs at halftime 29–27, and the game was fairly even through the first 20 minutes. St. John's received scoring from a vast amount of people, which was tough for the Georgia defense to deal with. But the Bulldogs had an answer in the form of Fair, who played a lights-out game for his team. In the second half, Georgia kept up with the sharpshooters from the Big East and were led by Fair's 27 points. The Bulldogs were able to score 43 second-half points to upset St. John's 70–67 and advance to the Elite Eight. Sure, No. 1 seed St. John's was tough to handle. But the next opponent? North Carolina, a team that could have made a strong argument that it should've been a No. 1 seed.

The Tar Heels that season were led by none other than Michael Jordan, the man who would go down as the greatest to ever play the sport of basketball. Sam Perkins, Brad Daugherty, and Matt Doherty were also in North Carolina's starting lineup, making it one of the better teams of that season. But Georgia got a balanced offensive effort to match North Carolina's output. Jordan lit up the stat sheet as usual with 26 points and six rebounds, but that was to be expected. For Georgia it would be James Banks' turn to come up big just two days after Fair helped deliver a win against St. John's. Banks exploded for 20 points on 7-of-10 shooting to aid the Bulldogs in what was an 82–77 win. Vern Fleming and Gerald Crosby both contributed 17 points apiece with Georgia shooting a staggering 56.1 percent from the field.

This win punched Georgia's ticket to the Final Four for the first time in school history. The 1983 Final Four was held in Albuquerque, New Mexico, and it was a big enough deal for the Bulldogs that mascot Uga IV made the trip out west to attend the festivities.

Georgia drew N.C. State in the national semifinal, and Houston and Louisville met in the other game. Houston and Louisville were two heavyweights that season who were expected to be in the Final Four. Georgia and N.C. State were both Cinderella stories. Although the Bulldogs did wind up a No. 4 seed thanks to an SEC Tournament run, their standing was very much on the bubble before winning the conference title. N.C. State, on the other hand, didn't have a shot at all without winning the ACC Tournament. But March was made for moments like this, and N.C. State defeated Wake Forest 71–70 in the opening round to set up a showdown against North Carolina. The Wolfpack took their rivals to overtime and eventually beat the Tar Heels 91–84 to advance to the finals. There, N.C. State would play a Virginia team led by Ralph Sampson and Othell Wilson. On paper N.C. State didn't have a chance. But the Wolfpack got it done, defeating the Cavaliers 81–78 to earn entry into the NCAA Tournament. A No. 6 seed in the West, N.C. State needed overtime to defeat No. 11 seed Pepperdine in the first round. Then it won 71–70 against No. 3 seed UNLV in the second round. In the regional semifinal, N.C. State defeated No. 10 seed Utah 75–56. This set up an Elite Eight matchup between N.C. State and Virginia, one the Wolfpack would again win 63–62.

To this day N.C. State's run to the Final Four is one of the most improbable to ever take place in the NCAA Tournament. And at this stage, it was Georgia standing in the Wolfpack's way. Georgia did not get out to a great shooting start and fell behind 12–6 in the game's first five minutes. The Bulldogs cut the Wolfpack's lead to 12–10, but N.C. State closed the first half with a 21–12 run to lead 33–22 at the break. N.C. State's scoring barrage continued after halftime. The Wolfpack got out to a 55–41 lead, and the lead stayed in double digits until there was under three minutes to go. Gerald Crosby was able to record a steal and feed Fleming for a layup to cut the N.C. State lead to 11 with 2:31 to play. N.C. State's Thurl Bailey missed a free throw, and Georgia capitalized on a Heard bucket combined with a foul. Heard missed the free throw, and Georgia came up with two offensive rebounds on the same possession. But both putbacks were missed before N.C. State corralled the ball. With N.C. State missing and Crosby converting a layup, the aforementioned possession turned out to be a killer. Instead of trailing by four, the N.C. State lead was still six. Fouled at the other end, Bailey made one of his two free throw attempts before Fleming cut the lead to five on a made shot at the basket with 1:32 to play. Georgia stayed aggressive, trying to come up with steals before fouling. But the Wolfpack made enough free throws to keep the Georgia comeback at bay. N.C. State would defeat Georgia 67–60. That set up a showdown for the ages with Houston, which had beaten Louisville 94–81 in the other national semifinal.

Of course, everyone knows what happened from here. N.C. State played an instant classic with the behemoth that was Houston. But as Dereck Whittenburg's prayer from 30 feet was falling short, Lorenzo Charles leaped up to grab it and dunk it through the hoop to give N.C. State a 54–52 upset against the Cougars. Although Georgia didn't win it all that year, it came awfully close to doing so against an incredibly tough slate. In wins against St. John's and North Carolina, it defeated two-time Olympians Chris Mullen and Michael Jordan, both

GEORGIA'S OTHER TOURNEY TEAMS

Georgia's entry into the 1983 NCAA Tournament, in which it reached the Final Four, marked the first time in school history it had even been in the big dance. Since and prior to the 2016–17 season, Georgia has been to the NCAA Tournament 11 additional times.

1985: No. 6 seed Georgia defeated No. 11 seed Wichita State 67–59 in the first round, lost to No. 3 seed Illinois 74–58 in the second round. (This appearance was later vacated due to NCAA sanctions.)

1987: No. 8 seed Georgia lost to No. 9 seed Kansas State 82–79 in overtime in the first round.

1990: No. 7 seed Georgia lost to No. 10 seed Texas 100–88 in the first round.

1991: No. 11 seed Georgia lost to No. 6 seed Pittsburgh 76–68 in overtime in the first round.

1996: No. 8 seed Georgia defeated No. 9 seed Clemson 81–74 in the first round, defeated No. 1 seed Purdue 76–69 in the second round, lost to No. 4 seed Syracuse 83–81 in overtime in the Sweet 16.

1997: No. 3 seed Georgia lost to No. 14 seed Chattanooga 73–70 in the first round.

2001: No. 8 seed Georgia lost to No. 9 seed Missouri 70–68 in the first round.

2002: No. 3 seed Georgia defeated No. 14 seed Murray State 85–68, lost to No. 11 seed Southern Illinois 77–75. (This appearance was later vacated due to NCAA sanctions.)

2008: No. 14 seed Georgia lost to No. 3 seed Xavier 73–61 in the first round.

2011: No. 10 seed Georgia lost to No. 7 seed Washington 68–65 in the first round.

2015: No. 10 seed Georgia lost to No. 7 seed Michigan State 70–63 in the first round.

of whom were on the famous Dream Team in 1992. That 1982–83 Georgia team will go down as the best ever in Athens based on what it accomplished.

Learn About Landers' Lady Dogs

On March 7, 1979, a letter addressed to Vince Dooley arrived in the mail from a man named Andy Landers. To this point Landers had been a women's basketball coach at a small school, having led Roane State College in Harriman, Tennessee, to an 82–21 record in only four years. After beginning that job at the young age of 22, Landers had bigger and grander dreams.

In his letter to Dooley, Landers wrote how he wanted to be the one to build the Georgia women's basketball program from scratch. With programs around the country launching women's teams, Landers had confidence in himself to start a team at Georgia from the ground up. "For the past couple of years, I have been possessed with the idea that the University of Georgia should feature the outstanding women's basketball program in America," Landers wrote in his letter to Dooley. "Georgia has the potential necessary to achieve this recognition, and my ultimate goal in coaching is to take a major college basketball program and build it from the ground up into an immediate national power."

Dooley was so moved by the letter that only six weeks later Landers was introduced as the first full-time women's basketball coach in school history.

Growing up in rural Maryville, Tennessee, Landers knew from a young age that he wanted to be a head basketball coach. He grew to love the sport, considering it was one he could play at any time by himself. Even with no one around, Landers could get his basketball and shoot some hoops by himself. "I was in sixth grade when I decided that's what I wanted to do," Landers said. "A lot of it had to do with the fact that I had an uncle, A.J. Wilson, who coached at one of the county high schools and had incredible success with both football and basketball. Sometimes experiences like that just stick with you."

Before Landers became the head coach at Georgia, the Lady Dogs had four part-time coaches work with the team. Flossie M. Love (1973–74), Elsa Heimerer (1974–77), Dave Lucey (1977–78), and Carolyn Lehr (1978–79) all coached teams at Georgia before Landers came along. Landers was an impressive candidate in Dooley's eyes. But it's unknown if anyone could have predicted what kind of coach Landers would become at the university.

In only his second season, Landers' Lady Dogs won the NWIT and concluded the year with a 27–10 record. A year later, in 1981–82, the Lady Dogs reached the NCAA Tournament in the first year the women's game featured one. Georgia would lose in the first round to Arizona State, but that would only set the stage for the next year's excellent season.

Georgia would earn a No. 2 seed and face No. 1 seed Tennessee in the Elite Eight of the 1983 NCAA Tournament. It was a hard-fought game, and the Lady Dogs had to squeak one out against the Lady Vols 67–63. Georgia advanced to the Final Four for the first time in the same year the men's team made the Final Four of its tournament, too. The Georgia program became the first one to have its men's and women's teams reach a Final Four in the same year.

Landers remembers trying to keep up with the men's team while preparing his team for the women's tournament games. "It was wild to watch and to experience, and all the while it was going on, I remember how exciting it was, but I couldn't get caught up in it because we were working on the other end to stay above water and get where we wanted to go," Landers said. "We're having to follow each other, trying to get scores. Of course, all the games weren't on television back then, and that was difficult. I remember when they were playing, and we weren't. A lot of the time we were practicing or traveling and getting back to the hotel or getting on the bus and trying to find out a score."

Many years later Durham didn't know Georgia was the first to get both the men and women in the same Final Four. He was just ecstatic both programs were able to have such great seasons. "It was their first trip, and I know it was our only trip, and there were a lot of people talking about Georgia basketball going to the Final Four," Durham said. "It's nice to be first in anything. Naturally, we were really happy for our players. Coach Landers and I had been friends ever since he came to Georgia. We were real close and still are, so I followed the women's team; we practiced in the same facility and got to know them. It was a total team when you talked about basketball with the men and women. There was no real separation, and we were all just thrilled for each other."

But like the men, the women would lose in the national semifinal to the team that would go on to win the championship. Southern California proved to be too much and won in a blowout before going on to defeat Louisiana Tech in the title game.

But that tournament put Landers and the Georgia women's basketball team on the map. A year later, the Lady Dogs were back in the Elite Eight. A year after that, in the 1985 NCAA Tournament, Georgia advanced all the way to the NCAA Championship Game. To get to the title game, Georgia had to beat Tennessee Tech, UCLA, Long Beach State, and Western Kentucky. The stars for Georgia that season were Teresa Edwards and Katrina McClain, and the two combined for 52 points in the semifinal win against Western Kentucky.

In the national championship against Old Dominion, Georgia's defense did a great job holding the Monarchs to 38 percent shooting from the field. But the Monarchs were too good on the boards, pulling down 57 rebounds to Georgia's 30. That proved to be the difference as Old Dominion defeated Georgia 70–65.

The NCAA Tournament run continued a year later, as Georgia reached the Sweet 16. In fact, Landers' teams made the NCAA Tournament in every year of its existence except for 1992, 1994, and 2015. Landers' Lady Dogs reached the Final Four in back-to-back years in 1995 and 1996. Earning a No. 3 seed in 1995, Georgia defeated Indiana, Louisville, N.C. State, and Colorado to get to the Final Four. But the Pat Summitt-coached Tennessee Lady Vols would prove too much in the national semifinal. The following year, Georgia made it back to the national championship as a No. 2 seed after running through St. Francis, Oklahoma State, Stephen F. Austin, Louisiana Tech, and Stanford.

Georgia was matched up against Tennessee, and the Lady Dogs had defeated the Lady Vols earlier in the year. Landers also had Saudia Roundtree on his team, a guard who won the Naismith College Player of the Year. But Georgia was unable to get it done in its return trip to the national championship, falling to Tennessee 83–65. Landers would reach the Final Four one more time in 1999, in which his team was defeated by Duke.

Although Landers was never able to win a national championship, the accomplishments he had at Georgia were exceptional. Building a team from scratch, Landers put together a 862–299 (.742) record in 36 years at Georgia, which included seven SEC championships, four SEC Tournament titles, and 31 NCAA Tournament appearances. Including his time at Roane State College, Landers' career spanned 40 years with a 944–320 (.747) career record.

Landers retired after the 2015 season, stepping down from the program he built from the ground up. "I feel blessed to have had the privilege of working at the University of Georgia for the past 36 years," Landers said. "Athens is a wonderful community where I have raised my family and had the unwavering support of my wife Pam, my daughter Andrea, and my son Drew. I appreciate the support of a wonderful Bulldog Nation, our loyal fans, and the Fastbreak Club members. I owe a special thanks to coach Vince Dooley for entrusting me with the challenge of building a successful program 36 years ago and to Greg McGarity for continuing that trust and support. A big thank you to Hugh Durham for being a young coach's mentor,

Golden Teresa Edwards

Growing up in Cairo, Georgia, Teresa Edwards was routinely getting the best of the boys on the basketball court. She'd often tell her parents she was staying late at school to help her teachers—only to get some extra time practicing the sport she loved.

Her dedication earned her a spot on the University of Georgia's basketball team, where head coach Andy Landers had plans to utilize her in a major way. Arriving on campus in 1982, Georgia immediately turned into a powerhouse, and the Lady Dogs advanced to the Final Four in both 1983 and 1985. The 1985 team made it to the National Championship Game, and Edwards scored 30 points in the Final Four win against Western Kentucky.

An unselfish player, Edwards, whose No. 5 jersey has been retired by the program, still holds the Georgia record for career assists with 653. While Edwards was still in college, she began competing for the U.S. National Team and represented the United States in five consecutive Olympics from 1984 to 2000. During that time she helped the U.S. win four gold medals in five tries. The lone miss was a bronze medal in 1992.

Edwards was inducted into the Women's Basketball Hall of Fame in 2010 and recognized for being the most decorated player in the history of the sport. A year later in 2011, Edwards was inducted into the Naismith Memorial Basketball Hall of Fame. "It doesn't get any better than this," Edwards said. "There's no other place to go. My first hero was Dr. J, and my basketball hero is Michael Jordan. This all started with the boys in Cairo letting a girl play with them, and now this girl is being inducted into a Hall of Fame alongside the greatest men's players of all time. So many people played a part in my journey, and I hope each and every one of them knows how much I appreciate them. I feel like a kid all over again and I'm a little nervous, too. It's like I'm going to be on the grandest of stages. I think I belong, but that doesn't mean I'm not nervous about being there."

to Presidents [Frederick Corbet] Davison, [Charles Boynton] Knapp, [Michael] Adams, and [Jere] Morehead for their guidance and leadership, to all my former and present staff members and coaches who worked tirelessly to help make the success that we have a reality.

"But most of all, I want to thank each and every player for committing to the challenge of being the best they could be, because in so doing they contributed to and established a tradition that fewer than a handful can match. They created a program that ranks among the most elite nationwide. I want to say once more that each and every honor that has come my way is the result of unselfish individuals who believed their team and the name on the front of their jersey was more important than the name on the back. Once again, thanks to everyone who has contributed to and supported Georgia basketball. Just like this university, you're special."

Take Pride in Tubby's Two Years

If Georgia was going to fire the architect of the program in Hugh Durham, it needed to have a great replacement ready to take over. They found one in Tubby Smith, who had done an impressive job building Tulsa into a competitive team. A young up-and-comer in the 1990s, Smith turned Tulsa into a Missouri Valley Conference champion in 1994 and 1995 and reached the Sweet 16 of the NCAA Tournament in both of those years.

Therefore, it made sense for Georgia to make a run at Smith once it made the call to fire Durham. Smith accepted and began the process of trying to take Georgia to a step higher than Durham had established during his 17 years with the program.

It didn't take long for Smith to get the ball rolling in Athens. Smith's squad opened the 1995–96 season 10–1 and immediately looked like they'd be a tough out during SEC play. But a four-game losing stretch in January diverted those plans, and the Bulldogs finished the regular season 18–8. Although Georgia was stomped by Mississippi state 86–68 in the second round of the SEC Tournament, the Bulldogs still earned entry into the NCAA Tournament in Smith's first season. And this is where the excitement began. As a No. 8 seed, the Bulldogs knocked off ninth-seeded Clemson in the first round 81–74. Facing No. 1 seed Purdue in the second round would be a tougher test, one would think. But the Bulldogs got a superb game from center Terrell Bell, who went 5-of-5 from the field and 5-of-7 from the free throw line for 15 points. Carlos Strong also put in a 17-point performance in the win. The upset moved Georgia to its first Sweet 16 since its 1983 Final Four run. There, the Bulldogs would face Syracuse in a thrilling overtime battle. Shandon Anderson dropped 25 points and Pertha Robinson scored 21 in an 83–81 Syracuse win. Syracuse would eventually advance to the national championship, where it lost to Kentucky.

After the Sweet 16 season, excitement was back where it was in the early 1980s for Georgia basketball. And Smith would deliver with another strong coaching performance for the Bulldogs. This time Georgia was much more on the map and entered the NCAA Tournament as a No. 3 seed. But the Bulldogs were upset by a Chattanooga team that shot 54.3 percent from the field in the first round.

Smith's two years were remarkable in Athens, but it was evident he had bigger dreams ahead. A former assistant at Kentucky, coaching the Wildcats was a dream job for Smith. And it just so happened that after the 1996–97 season, Rick Pitino elected to move on to the NBA's Boston Celtics, which left the Kentucky job open. Smith was offered and accepted. And like he did at Georgia, Smith won immediately at Kentucky. But at a place like that, he didn't just take the Wildcats to the Sweet 16. He won Kentucky a national championship in his first season.

Relive the Turbulence of the Tornado Tournament

The reality is that Georgia did not field a good basketball team during the 2007–08 campaign. The Bulldogs finished the regular season with a record of 13–16 and were coming off a 14-point loss to Mississippi. Head coach Dennis Felton was firmly on the hot seat. Finishing 4–12 in the SEC East, Georgia was given the SEC East's sixth seed. No one thought Georgia had a chance to win a game in the SEC Tournament—let alone the whole thing—that season.

And to start things off, the Bulldogs had to face Ole Miss, the team that just demolished them, in the first round at the Georgia Dome. On the opening Thursday of the tournament, the two teams went to overtime to settle the score. With the game tied, Georgia guard Corey Butler drove down the court and found center Dave Bliss for a bank shot to win the game. The Bulldogs stayed alive and were to play Kentucky the next night, March 15, 2008.

That's when things got crazy.

Georgia and Kentucky were the late game, which would take place after Alabama and Mississippi State wrapped up in the Georgia Dome beforehand. But the Crimson Tide sent the game to overtime thanks to a Mykal Riley three-pointer at around 9:30 PM. That put the start of Georgia and Kentucky on hold. With less than three minutes to go in overtime, a loud banging could be heard from the roof of the Georgia Dome. The scaffolding and lights then started to sway back and forth. Players diverted their attention from the floor to what was going on, and fans began to rise out of their seats. No one was certain in the moment what was happening, but it sounded serious. Therefore, the game was put on hold, and everyone moved into a safer location. During this time SEC officials were told a tornado had hit the Georgia

Sundiata Gaines holds up the MVP trophy after Georgia defeated Arkansas 66–57 during a miraculous run, which included playing two games in the same day, through the tornado-stricken 2008 SEC Tournament. (AP Images)

Dome. For a storm like that to touch down in an urban area like Atlanta was an extremely rare occurrence.

On the fly the SEC began getting information about the weather outside and was told that at around 10:30, an hour after the Alabama-Mississippi State game stopped, that there was a limited time frame of calm weather to where the remainder of the game could safely be played. So the game resumed then, and Mississippi State went on to win 69–67. But now the SEC had a bigger question at hand: what to do about the Georgia-Kentucky game?

With the threat of additional inclement weather coming in, the game was postponed to Saturday. On top of that, the Georgia Dome sustained damage and would be unable to support the rest of the SEC Tournament. The first choice to relocate was Philips Arena, but it was unavailable due to another event scheduled. The second choice was to go to Georgia Tech, which agreed to host the remainder of the SEC Tournament. So at least a venue was established.

But since the Georgia-Kentucky game was postponed, the winner of that game would have to play twice in the same day. On top of that, only 400 friends and family of players and staff for each school were allowed into the tournament at Georgia Tech. That meant those who paid for SEC Tournament tickets were no longer able to watch their team. Given how many Kentucky fans had been present at the Georgia Dome, the Wildcats no longer had that advantage.

Still, Kentucky had every on-court edge. But the Bulldogs came out swinging and raced out to an early lead. The Wildcats were able to claw back and even things out and caught a huge break when Georgia's best player, point guard Sundiata Gaines, fouled out in the second half. That brought in freshman guard Zac Swansey, who hadn't played much during the year. Georgia was able to take Kentucky to overtime with the score tied 50–50 at the end of regulation. Not much scoring was done during the extra period before Ramel Bradley hit a jump shot that rattled around before falling through the hoop with just more than eight seconds left to play to put Kentucky up 56–54. Georgia then called timeout to set up a play.

The original play call was simple. Swansey was to dribble the ball up the floor and get three-point specialist Billy Humphrey a look on a handoff. And as the play was materializing, it was open. But Swansey pivoted into a spin move and shot the three-point attempt himself. Swansey's freestyling paid off because his shot went in and gave Georgia a 57–56 lead with 1.2 seconds to go. Kentucky was unable to pull off a miracle and actually committed a foul followed by a technical foul to give the Bulldogs three more free throws. Georgia won 60–56 and advanced to the SEC Tournament semifinals against Mississippi State to be played later that night. Georgia players were administered intravenous fluids to aid in the recovery. "If we acknowledge the fact that we just played a game and we're tired, then we're gonna lose," Bliss said. "And we're not going to be able to beat this team that slept all day and is already more talented than us. What's stronger—your excuses or your desire?"

Georgia got out to a fast start against Mississippi State, but fatigue eventually set in during the second half. And then with 7:18 remaining, Gaines fouled out. It sure looked like the end of the road for Georgia. But with Gaines out, this time it was Humphrey who stepped up to the occasion and started knocking down shots. With 1:23 to play, Humphrey rose over a defender and knocked down a long two-pointer to put Georgia up 61–60. Georgia would go on to win 64–60 and advance to the SEC Tournament Championship Game.

A miracle was occurring.

Facing Arkansas in the title game, Georgia opened hot on a 22–7 run to start. The Razorbacks were able to get back into it and only trail 36–26 at the half. For the first 15 minutes of the second half, the Bulldogs held a sizable lead and kept thwarting off every run the Razorbacks tried to put together. But they could only do so for so long.

Arkansas went on a 14–3 run to cut Georgia's lead to 56–53 with 4:21 left to play in the game. But Georgia's grit was too much in the end.

The Bulldogs came up with three offensive rebounds on a possession that Albert Jackson finished with a dunk to go up 58–53. Humphrey then hit a three-pointer a little later to put Georgia ahead 61–53. The Bulldogs finished this game with a 66–57 win and celebrated on their archrival's home court, having punched their ticket to the NCAA Tournament. Nothing like this had ever happened before. It's likely nothing like this will ever happen again.

Climb into Fox's Den

Dennis Felton was on the hot seat after the 2007–08 regular season. Then he won an improbable SEC Tournament and reached the big dance. That gave him a reprieve. But Felton's team didn't show much improvement, which included losing to Loyola-Chicago, Western Kentucky, and Texas A&M-Corpus Christi during the non-conference portion of the season. The final straw was a January 28, 2009 loss at Florida by the score of 83–57. Felton was relieved of his duties, and assistant Pete Hermann took over for the remainder of the year. Georgia began its search for a new head coach.

Quite a few coaches were linked to the Georgia job, including then-Missouri head coach Mike Anderson, who reportedly took $600,000 less to stay with the Tigers. Then-VCU head coach Anthony Grant was also discussed, though university officials denied a meeting ever took place. Grant would wind up taking the head coaching job at Alabama.

But then-athletic director Damon Evans made what was seen as an outside-the-box hire at the time. With no reporter sniffing it out, Evans turned to Mark Fox, the head coach at Nevada from 2004 to 2009. With star forward Nick Fazekas on his roster, Fox's Nevada squads reached the NCAA Tournament three times from 2004 to 2007. But his teams weren't able to do so in his final two years at Nevada despite winning a total of 21 games in each season.

Still, Evans saw the upside Fox brought to the Georgia program. Fox is a man of integrity who won't bend the rules that a lot of NCAA basketball coaches do on the recruiting trail. From talking to folks, Evans found out that Fox was considered a renowned tactician who could out-scheme opponents to win with lesser talent.

Evans and Georgia signed Fox to a six-year contract with hopes of righting the ship. It only took two years for the Bulldogs to get back to the NCAA Tournament. After a 14–17 inaugural campaign, the Bulldogs led by Trey Thompkins and Travis Leslie won some big games that propelled Georgia into the big dance. The Bulldogs would come close to winning a first-round game against Washington, too, but fell 68–65.

Georgia, however, then saw Thompkins and Leslie declare for the NBA draft and was not in a position at the time to absorb that kind of loss of talent. Even with five-star freshman Kentavious Caldwell-Pope arriving, Georgia didn't have the surrounding cast to make up for the loss of talent. And boy, did Caldwell-Pope impress during his two years in Athens. A dead-eye shooter, Caldwell-Pope averaged 13.2 points per game as a freshman and a team-best 18.5 points per game as a sophomore. Although Georgia finished 15–17 overall in 2012–13, Caldwell-Pope was named the SEC Player of the Year. He turned pro and was drafted eighth overall by the Detroit Pistons.

The following season, in 2013–14, saw Georgia get back to the post-season and into the NIT. The year after Fox put together a team that made it back to the NCAA Tournament, thanks to a veteran front-court led by Marcus Thornton and Nemanja Djurisic. That season saw Georgia bounce back from a 3–3 start to win six consecutive games. The Bulldogs also recorded wins against Vanderbilt and Florida and played No. 1 Kentucky incredibly tough twice. Georgia received a No. 10 seed but got an incredibly tough matchup in the first round. Michigan State, a team that finished tied for third in the Big Ten regular season, somehow ended up paired with Georgia as a No. 7 seed. The Spartans would prove they should have received a better seed. But they sure faced a stiff challenge from the Bulldogs in the process. Down 13 at halftime, the Bulldogs rallied in the second half thanks to Charles Mann's 19 points. It wouldn't be enough as Michigan State won 70–63. The Spartans, naturally, ended up advancing to the Final

Four. Meanwhile, the Bulldogs were a wounded team that saw Kenny Gaines (foot), Yante Maten (concussion), and Juwan Parker (Achilles) all deal with injuries throughout the year. "If we were healthy, we could've been in the Final Four," Gaines said while looking back on that game. "That's the first thing that comes to my mind."

Djurisic and Thornton graduated, leaving a void in the frontcourt from a veteran standpoint. Georgia was on the bubble for the NCAA Tournament in 2015–16 but settled for an NIT berth instead. The same thing happened in 2016–17.

What Fox has done since his 2009 hiring has been remarkable. He took a bottom-feeding team in the SEC and turned it into an NCAA Tournament squad in two seasons. He's taken the Bulldogs to the big dance twice with three other NIT appearances mixed in. For the first time in Georgia history, one head coach has led the team to 20 wins three years in a row, which occurred from 2014 to 2016. The only other time Georgia won 20 games in three consecutive years came from 1995 to 1998 when Tubby Smith led the team the first two seasons and Ron Jirsa coached the third. Fox has also recorded four 20-win seasons overall, tying Hugh Durham with that feat.

Since Fox took over, the Bulldogs have placed three players in the NBA draft in Thompkins, Leslie, and Caldwell-Pope. Entering the 2016–17 season, 27 players of Georgia's basketball program earned undergraduate degrees. Appearing on a podcast with *The Atlanta Journal-Constitution*'s Jeff Schultz and WSB TV's Zach Klein, Fox said that when he took over the UGA basketball program, former university president Michael Adams told him it would be a 10-year rebuilding job. That was an astonishing fact to recollect, considering the lack of patience athletics programs tend to give coaches hired at Power 5 universities.

Given the state of the program Fox inherited, a long road to stability should have been expected. And over his first eight years, Fox has built a competitive SEC program battling for postseason berths. It's what he set out to do when he took the Georgia job from Day One.

BULLDOGS DRAFTED TO THE NBA

1950
Bob Healey, Syracuse Nationals (Round 8, 96th overall)

1951
Bob Schloss, Philadelphia Warriors (Round 3, 29th overall)

1953
Zippy Morocco, Minnesota Lakers (Round 5, 43rd overall)

1965
Jimmy Pitts, Philadelphia 76ers (Round 15, 102nd overall)

1970
Bob Lienhard, Phoenix Suns (Round 4, 61st overall)

1970
Herb White, Atlanta Hawks (Round 8, 133rd overall)

1973
Tim Bassett, Buffalo Braves (Round 7, 106th overall)

1973
Ronnie Hogue, Capital Bullets (Round 7, 116th overall)

1973
John Fraley, Buffalo Braves (Round 15, 195th overall)

1976
Jacky Dorsey, New Orleans Jazz (Round 2, 26th overall)

1977
David Reavis, Washington Bullets (Round 4, 83rd overall)

1979
Walter Daniels, Los Angeles Lakers (Round 3, 60th overall)

1980
Lavon Mercer, San Antonio Spurs (Round 3, 60th overall)

1982
Dominique Wilkins, Utah Jazz, traded to the Atlanta Hawks
(Round 1, third overall)

1982
Eric Marbury, San Diego Clippers (Round 6, 117th overall)

1983
Terry Fair, Indiana Pacers (Round 4, 72nd overall)

1983
Lamar Heard, San Antonio Spurs (Round 10, 225th overall)

1984
Vern Fleming, Indiana Pacers (Round 1, 18th overall)

1984
James Banks, Philadelphia 76ers (Round 3, 48th overall)

1985
Gerald Crosby, Golden State Warriors
(Round 6, 117th overall)

1986
Joe Ward, Phoenix Suns (Round 2, 31st overall)

1986
Cedric Henderson, Atlanta Hawks (Round 2, 32nd overall)

1987
Chad Kessler, Los Angeles Clippers (Round 5, 93rd overall)

1987
Dennis Williams, San Antonio Spurs (Round 5, 96th overall)

1988

Willie Anderson, San Antonio Spurs (Round 1, 10th overall)

1989

Toney Mack, Philadelphia 76ers (Round 2, 54th overall)

1990

Alec Kessler, Houston Rockets, traded to the Miami Heat
(Round 1, 12th overall)

1992

Litterial Green, Chicago Bulls, traded to the Orlando Magic
(Round 2, 39th overall)

1994

Charles Claxton, Phoenix Suns (Round 2, 50th overall)

1996

Terrell Bell, Houston Rockets (Round 2, 50th overall)

1996

Shandon Anderson, Utah Jazz (Round 2, 54th overall)

1999

Jumaine Jones, Atlanta Hawks, traded to the Philadelphia 76ers
(Round 1, 27th overall)

2003

Jarvis Hayes, Washington Wizards (Round 1, 10th overall)

2004

Rashad Wright, Indiana Pacers (Round 2, 59th overall)

2011

Trey Thompkins, Los Angeles Clippers (Round 2, 37th overall)

2011

Travis Leslie, Los Angeles Clippers (Round 2, 47th overall)

2013

Kentavious Caldwell-Pope (Round 1, eighth overall)

In doing so, Fox laid out a vision for those interested in playing for him at Georgia.

"They have to see that their dreams can come true—that they can win and play in the postseason, that they can play at the next level, that they can earn a degree," Fox said. "We're gonna have to earn that respect, and it'll take time."

Take Time for Taylor

For four years Joni Taylor got to see up close what it was like to run the Georgia women's basketball program. Studying under Andy Landers, she learned the ins and outs of how to properly manage a team from the first full-time head coach in team history.

The Georgia athletics program did its due diligence in trying to find a successor for Landers. But deep down Georgia knew it had the perfect candidate all along in Taylor—then Joni Crenshaw. On April 12, 2015, she became the second full-time head coach in program history.

The hiring was met with sound approval from Landers, her mentor. "Georgia basketball is in great hands," Landers said. "Coach Taylor is a person who has deep-rooted values and morals, which are two of the cornerstones of Georgia basketball's success. Her appreciation for the total development of young women is second to none, and her past experiences have prepared her for the challenges ahead. I am confident she will do extremely well. Joni has an excellent basketball IQ, is a tremendous recruiter, and is a terrific people person, but above all else, she is someone who young people will aspire to play for and enjoy that same experience."

It's never easy to replace a legend. But Taylor is a fiery and fierce competitor in her own right. Hired at 36 years old, Taylor is young enough to relate to today's youth, which certainly helps when on the recruiting trail. Taylor was a standout in her own right at Meridian High School in Mississippi. The 1997 Gatorade High School Player of the Year in her state, Taylor went on to play college basketball at

Alabama, where she appeared in two NCAA Tournaments and two WNITs. Before arriving as an assistant coach at Georgia, Taylor was an assistant at Troy (2002–05), Louisiana Tech (2005–08), Alabama (2008–10), and LSU (2010–11).

Taylor excelled immediately as Georgia's head coach, getting the Lady Dogs back into the NCAA Tournament after missing out on the big dance in 2015. Inheriting a senior-laden team, Georgia was a tough team for SEC opponents to face, especially in conference play. Georgia earned a No. 8 seed but lost to No. 9 seed Indiana 62–58 in the first round of the tournament.

The Lady Dogs finished 21–10, which marked only the 12th time in SEC history that a first-year head coach won 20 games or more in an inaugural season. The Lady Dogs' 12–1 start to the year marked the third best start an SEC coach has ever had in his or her first year. Taylor's first year didn't go unnoticed as she earned the WBCA Maggie Nixon NCAA National Rookie Coach of the Year Award, the Atlanta Tipoff Club's Whack Hyder College Coach of the Year Award, and the Advocates for Athletic Equity Rookie Coach of the Year honor. "She's someone a lot of the players can relate to," former Lady Dogs guard Marjorie Butler said. "She's somebody that is a little bit younger, and it makes her easy to relate to players, especially recruits too. She's extremely energetic. She's positive, she's upbeat. One thing we've been emphasizing is encouraging each other. I think those are things that have been brought in and incorporated because of her."

Taylor's second season featured some growing pains, considering the young and inexperienced team she brought back after losing a lot of senior leadership. Through the struggles there have been some bright spots, such as nearly knocking off South Carolina on the road. As Taylor places her own stamp on the Georgia women's basketball program, she knows she'll always have Landers to lean on when needed. Landers is still very much around the program and often spotted at the Georgia basketball facility. "He comes up to the office a lot," Taylor said. "He's very much still around and he's still very passionate about who we're recruiting. He's asked me in the last month about some visitors we were able to go visit, and I was getting some pretty poignant questions about who we're recruiting and how that was looking. He's very much involved and invested, and it's great to have him on speed dial."

One of the reasons Georgia's future is bright with Taylor is due to her recruiting prowess. For Georgia's recruiting class of 2017, Taylor was able to secure five-star guards Que Morrison and Gabby Connally, four-star guard Maya Caldwell, and four-star forward Malury Bates.

But the biggest addition Taylor, along with her husband Darius Taylor, welcomed to the Georgia program was the birth of her daughter, Jacie Elise Taylor, on November 3, 2016. With her daughter's birth coming shortly before the 2016–17 season began, Taylor was forced to miss the first few games of the year. But when she was able to return to lead her team, she was back in her coach's chair. "Darius and I can't express how blessed we are to be the proud parents of little Jacie," Taylor said. "She is a beautiful, healthy baby girl and has already brought so much joy to our lives. I want to personally thank everyone for all the prayers and encouragement you have shown us during this time. We are truly blessed and fortunate to be a part of the Georgia family, and are excited that our baby girl will be a part of such a special community."

On the Gridiron

Remember Georgia's First National Championship

With Wally Butts hitting his stride as Georgia's head football coach, there were great expectations entering the 1942 season. The Bulldogs returned their best player that season, a man by the name of Frank Sinkwich, who had just ended the 1941 season as a finalist for the Heisman Trophy. Guided by Sinkwich's leadership, Georgia was set for big things in 1942.

The Bulldogs were also coming off their first ever bowl game, a 40–26 win against TCU in the Orange Bowl. Sinkwich had a monster outing against the Horned Frogs, completing nine of his 13 passing attempts for 243 yards and three touchdowns while also rushing for 139 yards and another touchdown. Sinkwich entered the year as the Heisman favorite with Georgia meriting some serious conversation for a possible national championship.

In those days teams were all about running the ball. Although the forward pass would be a go-to sometimes, it wasn't used all that much. Butts, however, wanted to use it to his advantage as much as possible. Looking back, Butts was perhaps an innovator, a coach ahead of his time. He went to the pass a lot more than his counterparts and had Sinkwich, his halfback, deliver the ball to receiving targets in this manner.

The Bulldogs opened the 1942 campaign against Kentucky and put in one of their worst performances of the season. It was a sloppy game with Georgia turning the ball over four times. Sinkwich fumbled the ball early, which was converted into a Kentucky touchdown a few plays later. The Bulldogs, however, were able to block the extra point, which would be the difference in a 7–6 Georgia win. A week later Georgia faced a military program, Jacksonville NAS, and was able to come out with a 14–0 victory with the game being played in Macon, Georgia. Offensive mistakes were still present, but the defense came to play and shut out its opponent. From there, the Bulldogs were able to regroup and put together blowouts against Furman (40–7), Mississippi (48–13), Tulane (40–0), and Cincinnati (35–13). The Bulldogs now stood at 6–0 after a somewhat slow start with mighty Alabama coming to Atlanta for a big-time showdown.

Well over 30,000 fans came out to see Georgia and Alabama compete in Atlanta with the Bulldogs having every reason to defeat their SEC rival. The Crimson Tide, a year before, handed Georgia its only loss of the season, which took it out of the national championship conversation. The Bulldogs were also dealing with a drought against Alabama, having not secured a win over this foe since 1929. So there was a real desire for Georgia to come away with a win. But it sure didn't look good through the first three quarters. Entering the final period, Alabama held a 10–0 lead against Georgia and looked on its way to a fifth consecutive victory in this series. But that's when Sinkwich turned into the major Heisman contender he was. Sinkwich began delivering big passes down the field, converting one on a fourth down, to lead the Bulldogs for a touchdown. The Crimson Tide then turned the ball over and allowed Georgia to capitalize on it with the Bulldogs scoring another touchdown to go up 14–10. Georgia then got an insurance score with Andy Dudish returning an Alabama fumble 29 yards for a touchdown. Georgia won 21–10, which seemed near impossible after the first three quarters of the game. The Bulldogs improved to 7–0, moved to No. 1, and had their annual rivalry showdown with Florida up next.

But it wasn't a showdown. Florida never stood a chance in that game, and it became a laugher. Sinkwich and the Bulldogs jumped out to a big lead they never relinquished, defeating the Gators 75–0 in Jacksonville. To this day this is still the largest margin of victory in the series between the two teams. More than likely, this will never change in the history of this game. Georgia then got an easy blowout over Chattanooga by a score of 40–0, improving the team to 9–0.

The next test then came, and it wouldn't be easy—even if it came from a program that wasn't nationally ranked at the time. Auburn entered the game as a perplexing team. Remember that Florida team Georgia blew out 75–0? Auburn lost to the Gators. But Auburn had recently upset nationally ranked LSU and was riding high with confidence. The Tigers pulled out all the stops in this game. Having run the single-wing formation for much of the year, Auburn unveiled a T-formation and utilized many misdirection runs that confused the Georgia defense. On the other side of the ball, Auburn ran a defense Georgia hadn't seen in its preparation and thus forced Georgia to chase ghosts. Auburn held a 20–13 lead in the fourth quarter with Georgia having one last chance to tie the game. But Sinkwich was sacked and fumbled, and the Tigers returned it for a touchdown. Georgia lost the game 27–13, a stunning defeat at the time. The Bulldogs dropped from No. 1 to No. 5 in the national poll, hurting their national championship case in real time.

But the Bulldogs had a big chance to redeem themselves a week later against archrival Georgia Tech. With Georgia losing, the Yellow Jackets jumped up to No. 2 in the country. The winner of this game would head to the Rose Bowl, so a lot was riding on it. And it didn't take long for the Bulldogs to take their anger out on their hated foe. Sinkwich threw for 107 yards and ran for 72 in a 34–0 win. Charley Trippi chipped in a 38-yard touchdown throw and also scampered free for an 87-yard run. As a team Georgia racked up a staggering 492 total yards to Georgia Tech's 150. Georgia would head west to the Rose Bowl after picking up its first ever SEC championship.

Facing No. 13 UCLA, Trippi got the start ahead of Sinkwich, who won the Heisman Trophy, due to two sprained ankles. Trippi seized the opportunity and recorded 115 rushing yards. Butts made sure Sinkwich got in the game and utilized him as a short-field back when Georgia was close to scoring. Sinkwich couldn't get the Bulldogs in the end zone until the fourth quarter, which lengthened his team's lead to 9–0 thanks to an earlier safety in the game. Georgia totaled 373 yards and defeated UCLA in front of 93,000 fans in each team's first ever Rose Bowl appearance.

GEORGIA'S BOWL RESULTS

Listed below are Georgia's results in every bowl game through the 2016 season. The years listed are the seasons and not necessarily indicative of what year the game was played (i.e., if the game was played in the new year after that particular season).

1941: **Orange Bowl**, defeated TCU 40–26

1942: **Rose Bowl**, defeated UCLA 9–0

1945: **Oil Bowl**, defeated Tulsa 20–6

1946: **Sugar Bowl**, defeated North Carolina 20–10

1947: **Gator Bowl**, tied Maryland 20–20

1948: **Orange Bowl**, lost to Texas 48–21

1950: **Presidential Cup**, lost to Texas A&M 40–20

1959: **Orange Bowl**, defeated Missouri 14–0

1964: **Sun Bowl**, defeated Texas 7–0

1966: **Cotton Bowl**, defeated SMU 24–9

1967: **Liberty Bowl**, lost to N.C. State 14–7

1968: **Sugar Bowl**, lost to Arkansas 16–2

1969: **Sun Bowl**, lost to Nebraska 45–6

1971: **Gator Bowl**, defeated North Carolina 7–3

1973: **Peach Bowl**, defeated Maryland 17–16

1974: **Tangerine Bowl**, lost to Miami (Ohio) 21–10

1975: **Cotton Bowl**, lost to Arkansas 31–10

1976: **Sugar Bowl**, lost to Pittsburgh 27–3

1978: **Bluebonnet Bowl**, lost to Stanford 25–22

1980: **Sugar Bowl**, defeated Notre Dame 17–10

1981: **Sugar Bowl**, lost to Pittsburgh 24–20

1982: **Sugar Bowl**, lost to Penn State 27–23

1983: **Cotton Bowl**, defeated Texas 10–9

1984: **Citrus Bowl**, tied Florida State 17–17

1985: **Sun Bowl**, tied Arizona 13–13

1986: **Hall of Fame Bowl**, lost to Boston College 27–24

1987: **Liberty Bowl**, defeated Arkansas 20–17

1988: **Gator Bowl**, defeated Michigan State 34–27

1989: **Peach Bowl**, lost to Syracuse 19–18

1991: **Independence Bowl**, defeated Arkansas 24–15

1992: **Citrus Bowl**, defeated Ohio State 21–14

1995: **Peach Bowl**, lost to Virginia 34–27

1997: **Outback Bowl**, defeated Wisconsin 33–6

1998: **Peach Bowl**, defeated Virginia 35–33

1999: **Outback Bowl**, defeated Purdue 28–25 (OT)

2000: **Oahu Bowl**, defeated Virginia 37–14

2001: **Music City Bowl**, lost to Boston College 20–16

2002: **Sugar Bowl**, defeated Florida State 26–13

2003: **Capital One Bowl**, defeated Purdue 34–27 (OT)

2004: **Outback Bowl**, defeated Wisconsin 24–21

2005: **Sugar Bowl**, lost to West Virginia 38–35

2006: **Chick-fil-A Bowl**, defeated Virginia Tech 31–24

2007: **Sugar Bowl**, defeated Hawaii 41–10

2008: **Capital One Bowl**, defeated Michigan State 24–12

2009: **Independence Bowl**, defeated Texas A&M 44–20

2010: **Liberty Bowl**, lost to Central Florida 10–6

2011: **Outback Bowl**, lost to Michigan State 33–30 (3 OT)

2012: **Capital One Bowl**, defeated Nebraska 45–31

2013: **Gator Bowl**, lost to Nebraska 24–19

2014: **Belk Bowl**, defeated Louisville 37–14

2015: **TaxSlayer Bowl**, defeated Penn State 24–17

2016: **Liberty Bowl**, defeated TCU 31–23

Georgia finished the season 11–1 but would be unable to end the year No. 1 in the AP poll. Ohio State received that honor after a 9–1 season, even though the Buckeyes didn't play in a bowl game. In those days, however, AP votes were in before the postseason. But when claiming and sorting titles, nine of 11 polls named Georgia the national champion, which gave the Bulldogs their first consensus title. Given the lack of a playoff or bowl featuring the true No. 1 and 2 teams, both Georgia and Ohio State claim national titles. Many historians refer to Georgia as the national champion due to the consensus label, but those who strictly go by the AP claim the Buckeyes. So while Georgia is considered the consensus champs of 1942, the national title is technically disputed. Given Georgia's strength of schedule, the Bulldogs were deserving of the national championship. And it was a fitting way for Sinkwich to end his college career at Georgia.

Love the 1980 Season

If there was one word to describe Georgia's season in 1980, it would be "magic." What a magical year it was for a team coming off of a 6–5 season that ended without a bowl appearance. And in those days, when you needed a strong veteran running game, Georgia was going into the year not knowing exactly what it had in its stable.

Everyone around Georgia's team knew how good Herschel Walker was and what he could be down the road, most certainly including head coach Vince Dooley. But there was some hesitation to play him right away. In preseason practices Walker had been good but not spectacular. He wasn't someone who earned the starting job during camp. So entering the year, Donnie McMickens was named the starter, and Walker was down the depth chart. He'd play early but how much would be determined.

In Georgia's season opener at Tennessee, the Bulldogs went down 9–0 at halftime. Walker was given a couple of carries but hadn't done much with them. But given the other running backs hadn't either, Georgia decided to give Walker a shot to start the second half.

Head coach Vince Dooley is carried off the field after Georgia defeats Notre Dame to win the Sugar Bowl on January 1, 1981. (AP Images)

It wasn't until Georgia trailed 15–2 in the third quarter that Walker first showed his greatness. The Bulldogs drove down to the Tennessee 16-yard line to set up one of the most famous plays in Georgia football history. Quarterback Buck Belue gave the ball to Walker, who darted to his left and saw one person directly in front of him. That would be Tennessee safety Bill Bates. The legend of Walker was born as he trucked Bates, split two defenders, and trotted into the end zone for the score. Later in the game it was Walker again scoring a touchdown, helping give the Bulldogs a 16–15 lead. That would be the final score with Georgia escaping Neyland Stadium with a one-point victory.

Moving up from No. 16 to No. 12, the Bulldogs returned home for what would be the first of a five-game home stretch. Texas A&M came to town and didn't stand a chance with Georgia throttling the Aggies 42–0. Walker ran for 145 yards and three touchdowns in the game. Up next was Clemson, which was a much bigger rival in those days. Although Walker ran for 121 yards against the Tigers, it was defensive back Scott Woerner who emerged as the hero of the game. Woerner returned a punt 67 yards for a touchdown and later picked off a pass that he returned 98 yards. The deep interception return helped set up a touchdown for the Bulldogs. Down four late in the game, Clemson put together a drive to try and win the game. But Frank Ros tipped a pass that Jeff Hipp intercepted. The Bulldogs ran the clock out thanks to Walker's rushing ability as Georgia defeated Clemson 20–16.

A week later TCU came to town, and Georgia blitzed the Horned Frogs to the tune of a 34–3 victory. But Walker injured his ankle and didn't play beyond the first quarter. The defense dominated, however, totaling three fumble recoveries, two picks, and seven sacks. A bye week was up next with Georgia returning to conference play to take on Ole Miss. Walker was limited in the game with the injury, and Georgia scraped by to get a 28–21 win.

Walker healed up just in time for Georgia's game against Vanderbilt and ran roughshod against the Commodores. Walker had 202 yards at halftime and could have likely gone for 400 if he was kept in the game. But the Bulldogs were blowing out Vanderbilt, and, naturally, Dooley pulled him to prevent injury. After demolishing Vanderbilt, Georgia went on the road for only the second time that season to face Kentucky. Having worn red pants with the white away jerseys at Tennessee, the Bulldogs decided to go back to the silver britches for this one. Georgia would cruise to a 27–0 win with the highlight coming on a 91-yard pass from Buck Belue to Anthony Arnold. At the time it was the second longest offensive play in Georgia football history and today it's the fifth longest distance behind three plays going for 93 yards—David Greene to Tyson Browning against LSU in 2003, Greg Talley to Kevin Maxwell against Vanderbilt in 1989, Buck Belue to Lindsay Scott against Florida in 1980, and a 92-yarder from Kirby Moore to Randy Wheeler against Auburn in 1965.

Georgia was sitting pretty at 7–0 but knew an incredible challenge was coming its way with South Carolina. Walker was taking the world by storm, but South Carolina had a pretty good running back in George Rogers, who was a Duluth, Georgia, native. This game earned a national broadcast, which meant this would be the first time the entire country would be able to get a good look at Walker. Both running backs excelled on the big stage. But it was Walker who got the best of Rogers in the battle. Walker's most famous play of the game came in the third quarter. Walker hit a hole before sprinting to his right. Two South Carolina defenders ran toward him, appearing to have the angle to knock him out of bounds. But as they got close to Walker, the Wrightsville, Georgia, standout burned past them. A third South Carolina defender was approaching, too, on a similar angle but could not get to Walker in time. Walker's game-breaking speed torched the Gamecocks on that play for 76 yards and a touchdown. Walker's day would finish with 225 yards compared to Rogers' 174. Georgia would defeat South Carolina in front of a nationally televised audience 13–10 to improve to 8–0.

A week later Georgia was once again on national television. This time it faced hated foe Florida. Georgia moved up to No. 2 in the rankings with Florida checking in at No. 20. The game, as always, took place at the Gator Bowl in Jacksonville, and the world turned its attention to Walker and the Bulldogs. But Georgia had to avoid being emotionally spent from the South Carolina game. That's a worry of any coach coming off of a big win with another huge opponent up next. The Bulldogs got off to a great start with Walker running for a 72-yard touchdown against the Gators on their fourth offensive play of the game. Walker crushed Florida on the ground, running for 238 yards and shredding the defense time and again. Georgia held a 20–10 lead in the second half, but it wouldn't be enough of a cushion to put Florida away. The Gators scored 11 unanswered points and took a 21–20 lead. That set up the greatest play in the history of the Georgia football program. Facing a third and 11 from its own 7-yard line with less than two minutes to play, Belue took the snap from under center and rolled to his right to buy time under pressure. He stepped up and found receiver Lindsay Scott open in the middle of the field. Scott quickly turned—and turned the jets on. There was a ton of space on the left side of the field, which is exactly where Scott began churning his feet forward. Scott, who possessed elite track speed, hit the left sideline and sprinted to the end zone. The Georgia fans at the Gator Bowl exploded in jubilation with the Bulldogs going on to win that game 26–21. The win catapulted Georgia in the rankings, and the Bulldogs became the No. 1 team in the land with help from archrival Georgia Tech tying previously top-ranked Notre Dame 3–3.

It didn't get easier, however. A week later Georgia had another date with a rival; this time it was Auburn. And if history is a reminder, the last time Georgia was considered a consensus national champion—in 1942—Auburn was the team that gave the Bulldogs their only loss. In his book *Vince Dooley's Tales from the 1980 Georgia Bulldogs*, the former coach detailed how he brought in Frank Sinkwich to speak to the team before the Auburn game. Sinkwich, the Heisman Trophy winner in 1942, had a huge game in Georgia's lopsided 75–0 win against Florida. So when Georgia had to face Auburn, it was assumed the Bulldogs would roll. Instead, Auburn upset Georgia 27–13 and prevented the Bulldogs from an undisputed national championship. (Georgia is still considered the consensus national champion in 1942.) Although Walker was held to 84 yards against Auburn, Georgia was able to get a 31–21 win. Walker did ice the game with an 18-yard touchdown run late.

Georgia was now 10–0 and heading into its annual rivalry game against Georgia Tech, looking to complete an undefeated regular season. Although the Yellow Jackets tied Notre Dame earlier in the year, they stood no chance to knock off the Bulldogs. Totaling 205 yards and three touchdowns that day, Walker broke Tony Dorsett's freshman season rushing record. The No. 1 team in the nation, Georgia finished the regular season 11–0 and earned a Sugar Bowl berth. Win that, and they'd be national champions.

The Bulldogs' opponent would be Notre Dame, a team that was previously ranked No. 1 during the season. Falling to No. 6 after tying Georgia Tech, the Fighting Irish defeated No. 5 Alabama, which catapulted them back up to No. 2. But a regular-season-ending loss to USC knocked Notre Dame back to No. 7. Georgia entered the bowl season as college football's only unbeaten team, and a win would crown the Bulldogs champions.

But in between the regular-season finale and the Sugar Bowl came a distraction that was tough to avoid. Not too long before his team had a chance to earn a national championship, Auburn, Dooley's alma mater, came calling. Auburn was interested in Dooley to be its new head coach. The timing couldn't have been worse for the players with some later admitting in interviews that there was resentment that Dooley could possibly leave with the biggest game in school history on the horizon. But Dooley at least wanted to listen to what Auburn had to say. He detailed it in his book, *Vince Dooley's Tales from the 1980 Georgia Bulldogs*. "In the end I got back to Athens and looked at all of these pictures of Georgia players on the wall," Dooley wrote. "All my children had grown up in Athens. When we drove to the airport to go over there, [Vince's son] Derek was in the car crying. 'I hate Auburn!' To him, Auburn was a big rival, and at that age it was all or nothing, love or hate."

Through the ordeal the coaching staff hadn't been told much about what Dooley was doing. Hearing rumors that Dooley could leave were serious enough to begin an internal campaign to try and make defensive coordinator Erk Russell the new head coach. But despite the fact that Dooley played football at Auburn, was an assistant coach at Auburn, and his wife held an Auburn degree, all while his old roommate was now the governor of Alabama, Dooley realized his roots were in Georgia. He declined Auburn's offer and decided to stay at Georgia. Sure, it rubbed some of his players the wrong way. But eventually they got over it. After all, there was still a game to be played.

The world had come to realize the special talent Walker was. But in his biggest moment of his young career, Walker dislocated his shoulder

RUN LINDSAY!

When Georgia broke the huddle to line up for the third and 8 play at its own 7-yard line, Florida nose guard Robin Fisher allegedly told Georgia center Jeff Happe, "We are going to the Sugar Bowl." Happe didn't say anything in return and simply snapped the ball when he received the call to do so.

As Dooley wrote in one of his books, the play call was L-76. The flanker was asked to run a skinny post with the tight end crossing underneath. The split end would run a curl. Georgia actually ran a similar version of this play on a previous possession that nearly worked but fell incomplete. Georgia felt confident that it could find an opening over the middle this time around and pick up the first down.

After the snap, quarterback Buck Belue gave a slight play fake before setting his feet in the pocket. It didn't take long until he was forced to move to his right. A Florida pass rusher was barreling down at him, which caused him to scramble. And perhaps that pass rusher gets to Belue if not for a late block from Nat Hudson. Belue rolled right and started stepping up. That's when Belue noticed a wide open Lindsay Scott, sitting on the hash mark after curling his route. Belue threw the ball across the field to him for the completion and what would have been more than enough for the first down. Scott hopped to ensure he'd catch the ball and pivoted as quickly as anyone possibly could once his feet touched the ground again. His right foot swiveled to his right as he turned upfield to gain extra yardage. Scott's speed was too much for the Gators. He hit the angle to the sideline faster than any of the Florida defenders, outrunning four orange jerseys to the end zone. The play went for 93 yards and is known as the best in Georgia football history. It served as the miracle needed for the Bulldogs when hope was beginning to fade.

The play was further immortalized through the words of play-by-play announcer Larry Munson during his in-game call. "Florida in a stand-up five. They may or may not blitz. They won't," Munson began. "Buck back. Third down on the 8. In trouble, got a block behind him, going to throw on the run. Complete to the 25, to the 30. Lindsay Scott 35, 40. Lindsay Scott 45, 50, 45, 40. Run Lindsay! Twenty-five, 20, 15, 10, 5. Lindsay Scott! Lindsay Scott! Lindsay Scott!"

Pandemonium filled the airwaves before Munson continued about the play. "Well, if you want a miracle, we just got one," Munson continued. "Incredible play, Lindsay Scott caught the ball around the 40. There were a couple of players who had an angle. He knew that he had to run as fast as he possibly could. Well, I can't believe it. Ninety-two yards and Lindsay really got in a footrace, I broke my chair, I came right through a chair, a metal steel chair with about a five inch cushion. I broke it. The booth came apart. The stadium, well, the stadium fell down. Now they do have to renovate this thing. They'll have to rebuild it now. This is incredible. You know this game has always been called the World's Greatest Cocktail Party, do you know what's going to happen here tonight, and up at St. Simons and Jekyll Island, and all those places where all those Dog people have got these condominiums for four days? Man, is there going to be some property destroyed tonight! 26–21. Dogs on top. We were gone. I gave up, you did too. We were out of it and gone. Miracle!"

Scott was incredibly productive as a receiver at Georgia in every season statistically except his junior year. This was because he'd been in a motorcycle accident during the offseason and was forced to spend considerable time rehabilitating from it. Scott only scored one touchdown in 1980—that 93-yarder to beat Florida.

Scott would go on to have a great senior year in 1981, catching 42 passes for 728 yards and six touchdowns. He was selected by the New Orleans Saints in the first round of the 1982 NFL Draft.

early in the game. For a lot of players, this would be enough to sideline them for the remainder of the game. Walker told a team trainer to pop the shoulder back into place so he could get back in the game. The trainer did as he was told, and Walker continued to play. He was no longer able to be used as a receiver and could only carry the ball in one hand. But Walker showed the fierceness he competed with each week, along with the speed and power, to 150 yards on 36 carries against the Fighting Irish. Georgia would lead 17–3 and hold on for a 17–10 victory in the Sugar Bowl. Remember when Dooley almost left for Auburn? That certainly didn't matter now. Dooley decided to stay a Bulldog and was carried off of the Superdome turf on the shoulders of his players. Dooley delivered a starving Georgia fanbase its first undisputed national championship.

Learn About the Other Championship Seasons

Georgia has a direct claim to consensus national championships in 1942 and 1980 with the latter being the only one that is qualified as undisputed. But the Bulldogs do have claims to three other championships—whether the average college football observer wants to accept it or not.

In 1927 Georgia fielded a squad known as the "Dream and Wonder" team coached by Georgia "Kid" Woodruff. The Bulldogs jumped out to a 9–0 start to the season, which included an upset against No. 1 Yale. Georgia rose to the top of the polls entering its final game of the year against rival Georgia Tech. But it wouldn't be Georgia's day as the field in Atlanta was soaked following a rainstorm. Georgia Tech pulled off the upset 12–0, giving the team from Athens its only loss for the season. But even with the late-season loss, the Boand and Poling polls kept Georgia at No. 1. Illinois has long been considered the national champion of 1927, though Texas A&M started claiming a championship for this season in 2012.

The 1946 season might be the biggest and most legitimate gripe Georgia has when it comes to not claiming a consensus national title. After World War II, many players from Georgia's 1942 championship team returned to school, including famed running back Charley Trippi. He and the Bulldogs went undefeated at 10–0 in the regular season. But more amazingly, the closest any team got to Georgia during the first 10 games was Alabama, which fell to the Bulldogs 14–0. The Bulldogs then got a 20–10 win against North Carolina in the Sugar Bowl to cap off a perfect 12–0 season. Yet when it was time to name a national champion, the majority of the polls went with Notre Dame. Army also finished No. 1 in select polls. Both of those teams finished unbeaten but tied each other in a Game of the Century matchup during the middle of the season. Neither Notre Dame nor Army played in a bowl game. The Williamson poll is the only one that put Georgia at the top spot, which Georgia acknowledges in its media guide but doesn't outwardly claim.

In 1968 Georgia opened its season with a tie against Tennessee before reeling off five consecutive wins. The Bulldogs tied Houston 10–10 before going on to three more wins to finish the regular season 8–0–2. With two ties Georgia didn't have a shot at the AP or coaches' poll

Georgia's Conference Championships

In total Georgia has 13 conference titles, including 12 in the SEC. Prior to the 2017 football season, Georgia's 12 titles places it third in SEC history behind Alabama's 26 and Tennessee's 13.

Southern Conference
1920: 8–0–1

SEC
1942: 11–1 overall, 6–1 SEC
1946: 11–0 overall, 5–0 SEC
1948: 9–2 overall, 6–0 SEC
1959: 10–1 overall, 7–0 SEC
1966: 10–1 overall, 6–0 SEC
1968: 8–1–2 overall, 5–0–1 SEC
1976: 10–2 overall, 5–1 SEC
1980: 12–0 overall, 6–0 SEC
1981: 10–2 overall, 6–0 SEC
1982: 11–1 overall, 6–0 SEC
2002: 13–1 overall, 7–1 SEC
2005: 10–3 overall, 6–2 SEC

championships since Ohio State and USC were ranked first and second and meeting in the Rose Bowl. Penn State was No. 3 and facing Kansas in the Orange Bowl. Georgia was No. 4 and drew Arkansas in the Sugar Bowl. Georgia ended up losing to the Razorbacks with Ohio State knocking off USC and Penn State upending Kansas. Therefore, Ohio State is considered the 1968 champion. But the Litkenhous poll apparently thought more of Georgia than the other teams and placed the Bulldogs at No. 1 in its end-of-year poll. Like the 1946 season, Georgia acknowledges the national championship nod without claiming it.

Relive the Real National Championship Game

In the Southeast, or perhaps everywhere in the country outside of South Bend, Indiana, it was evident that the 2012 SEC Championship at the Georgia Dome in Atlanta was the true National Championship Game. The winner got to play Notre Dame, the nation's only undefeated team that regular season, in the BCS Championship Game. But given the Fighting Irish's weak schedule and how they played against those opponents, it was fairly obvious, even to the average fan, that by the end of the 2012 season, Alabama and Georgia had far stronger teams.

Midway through the year, it may not have looked like that. Georgia dropped a 35–7 blowout to South Carolina in a game in which the offensive line could not keep quarterback Aaron Murray upright. But as it is in many seasons, teams improve over time. From that moment Georgia defeated Kentucky, Florida, Ole Miss, and Auburn in consecutive weeks. The Bulldogs then closed the season with blowout wins against Georgia Southern and Georgia Tech.

But during this span, Georgia needed some help to climb back in the national title picture. After beating Georgia, South Carolina would cede the SEC East back to the Bulldogs with two consecutive SEC losses to LSU and Florida. Georgia also got some help when No. 1 Kansas State and No. 2 Oregon lost on the same weekend. This allowed Georgia to climb up to No. 3 just behind the new top teams in Notre Dame and Alabama. More importantly, it meant that if the Bulldogs won out, they'd be playing for a national championship title. This set the stage for Georgia and Alabama to play for the 2012 SEC Championship Game with the winner advancing to the BCS National Championship Game.

Georgia's defense, featuring outside linebacker Jarvis Jones and inside linebacker Alec Ogletree, came out on fire to start the game. The Bulldogs forced the Crimson Tide into two punts and a fumble, which Jones forced. It wasn't until Georgia's third offensive possession that it was able to get some points on the board. Running back Todd Gurley toted the rock for a total of 23 yards on the drive, and quarterback Aaron Murray hit Tavarres King down the field for a 33-yard chunk play. But the play of the drive came on a fourth-down fake punt. Tight end Arthur Lynch, acting as the punter's personal protector, took the snap and lofted a pass to defensive back Sanders Commings for a 16-yard first down. Two plays later Murray found tight end Jay Rome for a 19-yard touchdown to put Georgia up 7–0.

The teams traded punts before Alabama quarterback A.J. McCarron threw a pick to Commings. Georgia certainly held the early momentum against the Crimson Tide and looked to capitalize once again. But Alabama's defense stiffened up and forced Georgia into a three-and-out, and that was aided by a 10-yard holding penalty. Alabama's next possession was when its offense was finally able to get a spark. T.J. Yeldon took four carries in five plays for 26 yards. Then teammate Eddie Lacy took the ball and rumbled 41 yards down the field for a game-tying touchdown.

Hoping to score before the end of the half, Murray launched a deep ball, but it was intercepted by Ha Ha Clinton-Dix at the Alabama 18-yard line. Clinton-Dix returned it 35 yards to give the Crimson Tide a chance at points before halftime. McCarron then executed a five-play drive to set up a Jeremy Shelley 22-yard field goal. Alabama led Georgia at the half 10–7.

Georgia received the kickoff to start the second half and went right back to what worked all season long. Gurley carried the ball twice for nine yards with Murray finding King again for 31 yards. Three of the next plays were handoffs to Gurley, who totaled 31 yards on those carries. Facing first and goal at the 4-yard line, Gurley was once again fed twice with the then-freshman punching the ball into the end zone to give Georgia a 14–10 lead.

Alabama stalled out at the Georgia 32-yard line and brought place-kicker Cade Foster on the field to attempt a 49-yard field goal. The Bulldogs got a good push and blocked the attempt with the ball bouncing right to Ogletree, who took off 55 yards the other way for a touchdown. Georgia head coach Mark Richt ran down the sideline in excitement, and the Georgia bench jumped into jubilation.

But this was Alabama. By no means were the Crimson Tide going to lie down now that they trailed by 11 points. Yeldon ripped off a 31-yard run on Alabama's next drive to set up a 10-yard touchdown of his own. Alabama then got a two-point conversion to cut Georgia's lead to 21–18 with 4:19 to play in the third quarter. Alabama forced a Georgia punt and then got its ground game going even further. Lacy went for 32 yards, then for 15, and then for 14 yards, and Yeldon went for 13. Those were the highlight runs of the drive with Lacy eventually scoring a 1-yard touchdown to put Alabama up 25–21. But much like the Tide, Georgia wasn't about to roll over either. On the Bulldogs' next drive, Murray found King again for a 45-yard gainer to put Georgia down at the Alabama 12. Gurley would cap the drive off with a 10-yard touchdown run, giving Georgia a 28–25 lead.

Punts were then exchanged by both teams with Alabama getting the ball with 5:15 left in the fourth quarter. On the fourth play of the drive, McCarron found a streaking Amari Cooper down the field for a 45-yard touchdown to give the Crimson Tide a 32–28 lead. Put in bad field position on the ensuing possession, Georgia made the decision to punt the ball with 2:17 left to play. It was certainly a gamble, but one the Bulldogs felt they needed to take. It paid off as Alabama came up two yards short of a first down on three runs. The Crimson Tide punted the ball back to Georgia with 1:08 left to go.

Pinned at the Georgia 15-yard line and with no timeouts remaining, Murray found tight end Arthur Lynch for nine yards. Two plays later Gurley ran four yards for a first down. But for an instant, it looked like Georgia's season was over thanks to an Alabama interception. Murray threw the ball to receiver Chris Conley, who collided with Alabama safety Vinnie Sunseri with the ball bouncing to Dee Milliner for a pick. The Alabama sideline celebrated, thinking it had just won the game. But after an extended review period, it was determined the nose of the ball touched the turf and therefore wasn't an interception. Georgia re-took the field to continue its drive. Murray composed himself before the snap and then hit Lynch for a 15-yard gain on the right sideline. On the next play, Murray waited for King to break open before rifling in a ball in between two Alabama defenders for a 23-yard pick-up. King was hit hard by the opposition and stayed down momentarily. He eventually got up and ran off of the field to be tended to. Murray got his group the line of scrimmage at the Alabama 34-yard line and barked out instructions to his teammates. He received the snap with 30 seconds left to play and found Lynch over the middle for a 26-yard gain with Lynch carrying Sunseri for seven or eight of those yards. With it being a first down, the clock stopped for the ball to be re-set as Georgia ran to the line. Murray looked to the sideline and motioned to spike the ball—or at least seemed to be asking if that is what the coaching staff wanted him to do. Fifteen seconds remained in the game. Murray kept looking at the sideline, and it became apparent that the coaching staff wanted him to run a play instead. Murray relayed the call to his teammates in a total of four seconds of time before having the football snapped into his hands with nine seconds to go in the game. Murray had the matchup he wanted on the outside with Malcolm Mitchell in single coverage. The play was to hit Mitchell on a back-shoulder fade in the end zone. The reason Georgia didn't ask for a spike was to keep Alabama in the same defense. So it looked like the play was set up. But Alabama linebacker and future NFL first-round draft pick C.J. Mosley got his hand on Murray's pass and tipped it away from its intended target. The ball floated in the air and landed into Conley's arms. Before Conley could turn and run upfield or try to get out of bounds, he slipped five yards short of the end zone. It was a heartbreaking way for Georgia to end the game as it lost to Alabama 32–28.

Much debate has been made since that moment. A lot of people maintain Georgia absolutely should have spiked the ball in that situation to at least have the chance of two plays instead of one. But if the call from the sideline worked, the Georgia coaches would look like geniuses. It didn't, and the scrutiny came with the territory.

That game went down as the best that season saw. It was an instant classic that just might be the greatest SEC Championship Game ever played. Alabama gleefully celebrated its victory, which allowed it to play Notre Dame for the BCS Championship in Miami. Georgia would face Nebraska in the Capital One Bowl and win 45–31. As most of the nation expected, Alabama went on and annihilated Notre Dame by a score of 42–14. It was clear which two teams were the best by the season's end based on the epic SEC Championship Game Alabama and Georgia played against one another.

Hear the Redcoats Play

A hush comes over Sanford Stadium when the PA announcer directs the fans toward the South end zone. Fans begin to point as a trumpet soloist begins the first 14 notes of the "Battle Hymn of the Bulldog Nation," a slowed down version of Georgia's fight song "Glory" with cheers beginning to boom out. Accompanied by a video featuring a voiceover from former Georgia play-by-play broadcaster Larry Munson, the anticipation for another football game builds among a frenzied crowd. When that's over the band begins playing the traditional version of "Glory" with the team running onto the field. It's a tradition like no other at Sanford Stadium on gamedays.

The Redcoat Band plays before Georgia goes on to defeat Tennessee 41–14 in 2010. (AP Images)

The Redcoat Band is a beloved institution at the University of Georgia and is one of the more recognized marching bands in all of college football. Formed in 1905 as an extension of the on-campus military department, the band has grown from 20 to 400.

A nationally respected group, the Redcoats became the first SEC marching band to receive the coveted Sudler Trophy awarded by the John Philip Sousa Foundation. The Redcoats perform during the Dawg Walk, on the field before the game, and at halftime.

Hate the Yellow Jackets

The second verse in the fight song "Ramblin' Wreck from Georgia Tech" is something those who follow the Yellow Jackets, Georgia's biggest rival, yell at the top of their lungs when they sing it.

Oh! If I had a daughter, sir, I'd dress her in White and Gold,
And put her on the campus to cheer the brave and bold.
But if I had a son, sir, I'll tell you what he'd do—
He would yell, "To hell with Georgia!" like his daddy used to do.

That's hate. Clean, old-fashioned hate.

As the story goes, Georgia's fans heckled Georgia Tech's pretty good during the first ever meeting between the two football teams in 1893. The Georgia Tech Blacksmiths, as they were originally called, won 28–6 but the Red and Black faithful made sure to let the other team's supporters know how much they were resented. As the story goes, a Georgia fan even threw a rock at a Georgia Tech player on the field.

It wasn't long after that game that the fight song was written. Georgia Tech claims that one of its football players wrote the lyrics while the team was on its way to a game against Auburn. Point is, Georgia riled up Georgia Tech to the point one of its own players, even after a win, wrote a fight song with a jab at Georgia. That's how rivalries are born.

And Georgia returns the favor when the two schools play and the rally song "Glory" plays. At the last line of the verse, Georgia fans shout, "And to hell with Georgia Tech!"

This rivalry has featured two teams that hated each other from the start. Even before the teams ever played a game, there was contention. When Georgia first began its athletics program, its colors were old gold, black, and crimson. Dr. Charles Herty, the first football coach at Georgia, hated the idea of old gold as a color. In his mind old gold was similar to yellow, and yellow symbolized cowardice. After beating

Georgia that first time, Georgia Tech adopted old gold as an official color.

But after that inaugural game, Georgia would win five of the next six games against Georgia Tech. The other one ended in a tie. Historically, for the first 65 years, this was a fairly even series. Each team would go back and forth with mini-winning streaks. The longest Georgia Tech ever had on Georgia came from 1949 to 1956 when the Yellow Jackets recorded eight wins in a row over its hated archrival. This ate at Georgia—from head coach Wally Butts, to the players, to the alumni, and to the fans. So when Theron Sapp scored the only touchdown in the 1957 game to help Georgia defeat Georgia Tech 7–0, Sapp was carried off the field and celebrated as a hero. He had an excellent career outside of this achievement, but because he was a big reason why Georgia ended the losing streak, the university retired his jersey. Sapp has been affectionately referred to as the "drought breaker."

The two teams were in the Southern Conference and the SEC together as conference foes until 1964. That season former Georgia Tech head coach Bobby Dodd wanted the SEC to get rid of the 140 rule, which meant that member athletic programs could put 140 student-athletes on scholarship, but only 45 could be used for football. Some programs were releasing players from scholarships if they were unable to perform. Dodd didn't like this and sought to change the rule. A 6–6 vote, however, kept the rule in place, and Georgia Tech immediately left the conference.

Want to know how vital this decision turned out to be? Prior to the 1964 game between Georgia and Georgia Tech, the Yellow Jackets held a 27–26–5 lead in the series. Georgia then won 7–0 in 1964 to tie the series up. Including that year, the Bulldogs have since gone 39–14 against Georgia Tech in the seasons after.

There have been some great moments that show the kind of hate from these two rivals. In the early days, Georgia Tech kept Georgia from possibly getting an undisputed national championship in 1927 when the Yellow Jackets gave the Bulldogs their first and only loss of the season in the final game. Georgia and Georgia Tech played against each other during World War II, even though many of Georgia's stars were off fighting in battle. Later on former Georgia sports information director Dan Magill decided those two games—Tech wins of 48–0 and 44–0 in 1943 and 1944—would not count in Georgia's official record book. In 1942 after Georgia lost a shocker to Auburn, the Bulldogs took it out on Georgia Tech and smashed their rival 34–0. Georgia also blew out Georgia Tech 35–7 in its undefeated season of 1946. In 1978 Georgia quarterback Buck Belue entered the game with his team down 20–0 in the second quarter. He helped rally the Bulldogs to a 29–28 comeback win against their hated rival. When Herschel Walker was on campus at Georgia from 1980 to 1982, the Bulldogs never lost to Georgia Tech.

Like with any rivalry, there has been its share of controversy, especially in the last couple of decades. In 1999 Georgia was looking to win the game against Georgia Tech late. With the ball at the 2-yard line and both teams tied at 48–48 and with 13 seconds remaining in the game, Georgia running back Jasper Sanks took a carry up the middle and appeared down on the ground before a Georgia Tech player ripped the ball away from him. But the referee crew headed by Al Ford called it a fumble, giving Georgia Tech the ball and extra life in overtime. The Yellow Jackets went on to win the game, and Al Ford's referee crew was banned from officiating the SEC championship.

In recent years, there have been a ton of thrillers in this rivalry. In 2013 Georgia and Georgia Tech went to double overtime to settle the game, and the Bulldogs won 41–34. A year later in 2014, Georgia Tech defeated Georgia 30–24 in overtime, and Harrison Butker hit a 53-yard field goal with time running out in regulation. In 2016 Georgia led 27–14 in the fourth quarter but ended up dropping the game 28–27.

Although Georgia has owned the rivalry over the latter half of it, there are still likely to be some thrilling games against teams that continue to hate each other as much as they did back in the day—perhaps without the violence of throwing rocks at one another. Georgia fans still refer to Georgia Tech as the North Avenue Trade School and its fans as nerds. In reality, the rivalry that's been called Clean, Old-Fashioned Hate really isn't all that clean. There's just a lot of hate.

In an interview with journalist B.J. Bennett, former Georgia defensive lineman Jeff Owens described his hatred for Georgia Tech. "I am most definitely anti-Georgia Tech. It all goes back to the 2008 season, when we lost to Georgia Tech for the first time in about eight years," Owens said, referring to Georgia's winning streak over Georgia Tech from 2001 to 2007. "It was like the worst loss ever. We could have lost to a 1-AA opponent, maybe a Division II opponent, and it probably would have been the same. From my experiences it's all the same. We all hate Georgia Tech. People don't know this, but Georgia Tech has a replica of a Bulldog in their urinals. That's how big the rivalry is. Also, Georgia Tech players—seniors—get rings for beating Georgia, and the coaches get raises for beating Georgia. I hate Tech, everything about them."

Experience the World's Largest Outdoor Cocktail Party

During the weekend of a Georgia-Florida game in the 1950s, Bill Kastelz, the sports editor of *The Florida Times-Union*, witnessed a drunk fan walk up to a police officer and offer him a drink. An idea then popped into the head of Kastelz, who has since been credited with coining the nickname for the annual meeting between these two SEC foes. *The World's Largest Outdoor Cocktail Party.*

It's quite the scene in Jacksonville, Florida, each year the two teams go against each other. And it's been that way since 1933 when Jacksonville became the neutral-site location for this game annually. It's certainly a festive atmosphere the day before and the day of. It's treated like a vacation, and a lot of drinking takes place—from college students and alumni alike. A once-embraced moniker has since been dialed back out of concerns of binge drinking. But while it may not be promoted as such anymore, the festivities still take place.

One of the more remote routes to take when driving from Northeast Georgia down to Jacksonville is to take Hwy 15. This route takes you through Sparta, Sandersville, Tennille, Wrightsville (the birthplace of Herschel Walker), and Adrian before meeting up with Interstate 16. From there it's a westward drive until hitting Interstate 95, which takes you down to Jacksonville.

The return drive from the Georgia-Florida game on Highway 15 will take you by a barn in Tennille that has a message painted on it the next day. Depending on how the game went, it could be written in exultation. If the game went poorly for Georgia, the message could be of despair. After the 2015 loss to Florida, the message was, "Failed expectations...again."

Ross Smith has been the one painting the barn throughout Georgia seasons. He shares in the highs and lows the team's fanbase goes through. Smith has been doing this since 2000 with Georgia fans often stopping by the barn, which was once an old general store, and taking photos with it. The barn is painted more often than just the Florida game. But that weekend sees a lot more eyes on it due to the route taken for the road trip. After Georgia's 24–10 loss to Florida in head coach Kirby Smart's first season in 2016, Smith painted a message for the fans heading back home. "Trust the process," it read.

As for the football game itself, the origin of this rivalry is up for debate. Georgia lists the first ever game with Florida as taking place in 1904, a contest the Red and Black won 52–0. The University of Florida, as it's known today, claims that was a different institution that played in that game. The Gators claim Georgia's 1904 opponent was actually the Florida Agricultural College in Lake City, Florida. But Georgia points out the Florida Agricultural College was one of a few schools consolidated to later become the University of Florida.

Georgia's former sports information director Dan Magill said the 1904 game was most certainly the first in the rivalry. A 1941 edition of *Times-Union* backs him up by citing that particular game as No. 1. "That's where Florida was back then. We can't help if it they got run out of [Lake City]," Magill said.

That game in 1904 was played in Macon, Georgia, as the rivalry bounced around a bit. Only three times before 1933 was this game played in Jacksonville. Georgia won the rivalry's first seven games, as the two teams began to play on a more regular basis in 1915. Only once since 1926 has this game not happened, and that year was during the middle of World War II in 1943. The Bulldogs jumped out to a 24–5–1 lead in this series before Florida became more consistently competitive. But from 1952 to 1963, things didn't go so well for Georgia. The Gators flipped the rivalry and won 10 out of 12 games. Then Vince Dooley took over the Georgia program in 1964 and snapped a four-game losing streak to Florida with a 14–7 victory.

Under Dooley, the Bulldogs regained control of the series in the 1970s and 1980s. Dooley compiled a 17–7–1 record against the Gators, making their lives miserable year in, year out. This included two separate winning streaks of three and one of six from 1978 to 1983.

The tide turned again in 1990 when Steve Spurrier came back to his alma mater to coach the team. Spurrier had done the unthinkable and won a lot of games at lowly Duke, which made Florida look pretty smart in bringing on the brash former Heisman Trophy winner. And Spurrier's disdain for Georgia was evident from the start. Spurrier led the Gators to seven consecutive wins against Georgia from 1990 to 1996. After Georgia got one over the Gators in 1997, Spurrier's squads reeled off four more before he left for the NFL's Washington Redskins.

For all the success Georgia head coach Mark Richt had during his 15 years, one of his downfalls was the fact he went 5–10 against Florida. Spurrier went 1–0, Ron Zook went 2–1, Urban Meyer went 5–1, and Jim McElwain went 1–0 against Richt. The only Florida coach Richt had a winning record against was Will Muschamp, from whom he

Thousands flock to the World's Largest Outdoor Cocktail Party—the annual rivalry game between Florida and Georgia in Jacksonville, Florida—in 2012. (USA TODAY Sports Images)

took three of four games. McElwain then added another win against Georgia with a 24–10 victory in 2016.

Because of its dominance early on, Georgia still holds the all-time series lead at 50–43–2 prior to the start of the 2017 season.

The Georgia-Florida rivalry has seen its share of wild moments. It always seems the unthinkable happens in this series. In 1941 Frank Sinkwich played through the pain of a broken jaw with a device on his helmet to protect the injury. Despite the ailment Sinkwich scored 15 points in a 19–3 victory. This included a field goal from 27 yards out, which was seen as a major deal back in those days. Sinkwich totaled 31 carries for 142 yards and two touchdowns. Tom Lieb, the head coach at Florida that season, was asked what the difference in the game was. "Too much Sinkwich," he said.

A year later in Georgia's 1942 championship season, Sinkwich and Charley Trippi combined to score seven touchdowns in a 75–0 drubbing against the Gators. To date this is the biggest margin of victory in the rivalry. In 1966 Georgia faced Spurrier as a player. This was Spurrier's Heisman Trophy season, and he'd run away with the award fairly early on. But Georgia turned out to be his toughest foe that year, as the defense repeatedly disrupted him to the tune of three interceptions in a 27–10 win. Georgia defensive end Bill Stanfill spoke about growing up on a farm in Cairo, Georgia, during his College Football Hall of Fame speech. And he offered one anecdote of what it was like to bring Spurrier to the ground in a game. "Holding pigs for my dad to castrate was quite a challenge," Stanfill said. "I can't say that helped prepare me for football, but it sure did remind me an awful lot of sacking Steve Spurrier."

Georgia's 1975 meeting with Florida saw the two teams engage in a low-scoring affair. As a result Dooley decided to go with a trick play to try and fool the Gators. This was a rare occurrence for someone like Dooley, who, for the most part, kept things conservative. But this time Georgia called a reverse to tight end Richard Appleby around the end. Appleby, however, stopped and launched a pass to a wide open Gene

Washington, who finished the 80-yard play in the end zone, which ultimately gave Georgia a 10–7 win.

The best play in Georgia football history came against Florida in 1980. With the game coming down to the final minute and with Florida leading 21–20, quarterback Buck Belue took the snap and faked a handoff before rolling to his right to evade pressure. He stepped up and fired a dart to Lindsay Scott, who then pivoted to his right and ran to the open space on the left side of the field. Scott completed the 93-yard play to give Georgia a 26–21 win while keeping its national championship dreams alive.

In 1993 Georgia and Florida played a classic down-to-the-wire game in the rain and with controversy. Quarterback Eric Zeier got the Bulldogs down to the Florida 12-yard line and hit Jerry Jerman for a touchdown. But officials said the play didn't count because Florida called a timeout just before the snap. On the ensuing play, Florida committed pass interference, giving the Bulldogs one more play. Georgia was unable to score and lost 33–26.

Two games in 1994 and 1995 were ones to forget for Georgia. With Jacksonville Municipal Stadium under renovations, the games were moved to the two campuses. In 1994 the game was a 52–14 win for Florida in Gainesville. Florida won 52–17 a year later in Athens.

When Georgia scored its first touchdown against Florida in 2007, the entire team ran on the field to celebrate, drawing numerous flags from officials. Offensive lineman Trinton Sturdivant made highlight reels for a funky dance he did as a part of the orchestrated party. The idea was to set an emotional tone on the field, which was accomplished. Georgia used that early juice to defeat the Gators 42–30.

In 2012 when Georgia played for the SEC championship, its late-season surge got started against Florida. The Gators were undefeated and the second ranked team in the nation. Georgia was ranked 10th with a 6–1 record. The Bulldogs used stingy defense to limit Florida and got one of the biggest plays from outside linebacker Jarvis Jones in his career. With the Bulldogs leading 17–9, quarterback Jeff Driskel completed a pass over the middle to tight end Jordan Reed, who was running toward the end zone. But Jones hustled to the play and punched the ball out of Reed's arm. Georgia fell on the ball at the Florida 5-yard line, and that was its sixth forced turnover of the game.

Georgia and Florida have played plenty of classics, and there should be many more to come. Both teams and fanbases hate each other, and those strong emotions are probably why the weekend in Jacksonville is so much for fun for everyone involved. It's a neutral site atmosphere where folks can have a good time. In the mid-2000s, both Georgia and Florida wanted to separate themselves from the term "The World's Largest Cocktail Party" in an effort to curb underage binge drinking. The programs don't use the phrase anymore and neither do the CBS announcers when broadcasting the game. Although it's no longer the official name, it's still fondly referred as such by fans of both teams.

Revel in the Deep South's Oldest Rivalry

In 1892 Benjamin Harrison was the president of the United States, who then lost re-election to Grover Cleveland. Ellis Island had just started welcoming immigrants from Europe. Inventor Thomas Edison received a patent for the two-way telegraph. It was most certainly a long, long time ago. It also marked the year that Georgia and Auburn played their first football game against one another.

They don't call this "The Deep South's Oldest Rivalry" for nothing.

Georgia fielded its first team in 1892 and played two games. The first was a 50–0 romp against Mercer. The second came against Auburn in what turned out to be a colorful game between the two schools. Georgia brought a goat to the game to be its mascot, and the Auburn fans chanted to shoot it. With the game in Atlanta, the tension was palpable between the two teams. Auburn came away with a 10–0 win.

Although Georgia considers Georgia Tech and Florida as bigger rivals, that probably has more to do with the modern history of the game, and this matchup is the oldest. Auburn and Georgia have been meeting regularly since 1898 with the exception of three years. With World War I happening, the teams did not play in 1917 or 1918. Although Georgia fielded a team in 1943, even with World War II going on, Auburn did not. Those are the only exceptions this rivalry has seen.

This game predates each team's intrastate rivalries; Georgia did not play Georgia Tech, and Auburn did not play Alabama until the 1893 season. As far as college football rivalries are concerned, this is the eighth most played game in the history of the sport.

How important is this rivalry to those who have played in it? Take Rufus Nalley, who played football at Georgia for five seasons from 1892 to 1896. After graduation Nalley became an assistant for the team but caught a severe illness in 1902 that acted quickly. As the story goes, Nalley was bedridden and had a visitor tell him that Georgia had just snapped its four-year winless streak (two losses and two ties) with a 12–5 win against Auburn on November 27, 1902. The news brought a smile to Nalley's face. Later that day he slid into unconsciousness and died. The last time Georgia had beaten Auburn prior to the 1902 win? In 1896 when Nalley was in his final season with the team.

In 1916 a moment in the Georgia-Auburn game made national news. In muddy conditions the game was tied at 0–0 into the fourth quarter. Auburn decided to try a field goal from 40 yards out, which would seem inconceivable in those days given that there were no kicking specialists at that time. But Auburn back Moon Ducote lined up ready to kick a field goal. As he lined up for the try, holder Lucy Hairston took his leather helmet off and placed it on the ground, creasing the top of it to create a makeshift kicking tee. The ball was snapped, placed on the point of the helmet, and kicked through the uprights. The Georgia bench protested, but the referee pulled out his rulebook and said there was nothing in writing suggesting this was against the game's bylaws. The points stood, and Auburn won 3–0. This instance, along with others, caused the college game to force kicks to occur from the ground. Rulesmakers would allow for a one-inch rubber kicking tee in the late 1940s until those were once again banned on field goals and extra points in 1989.

The 1942 edition of the rivalry saw Auburn upset Georgia 27–13 in a game no one expected the Bulldogs to lose. Georgia was undefeated and coming off of a 40–0 win against Chattanooga. But Auburn came out with new schemes on both the offensive and defensive sides of the ball that Georgia wasn't prepared for. The upset occurred, keeping Georgia from being able to claim an undisputed national title. The Bulldogs, though, were still able to claim a consensus championship.

For whatever reason this game has featured a ton of late fourth-quarter plays to win games. Fran Tarkenton threw a touchdown in the final seconds of the 1959 game to give Georgia a 14–13 win against Auburn. In 1996 Mike Bobo threw a 30-yard touchdown to Cory Allen at the end of the fourth quarter to send the rivalry to overtime, and Georgia ended up winning 56–49 in four overtimes. Facing a fourth and 15 in 2002, David Greene lofted a pass up to receiver Michael Johnson in the left corner of the end zone. Johnson was able to come down with the ball over Auburn defensive back Horace Willis to defeat the Tigers 24–21.

Then, of course, there was the heartbreaker in 2013— the one known as "The Prayer at Jordan-Hare." Auburn led for most of the game and held a 37–17 lead when the fourth quarter began. That's when Georgia quarterback Aaron Murray went to work to try and lead his team to an improbable comeback. First, Murray drove down the field and found Rantavious Wooten for a five-yard touchdown. On Georgia's next possession, Murray hit tight end Arthur Lynch for a 24-yard touchdown with 5:59 left to play. Getting the ball back down six, Murray drove down to the 5-yard line. Facing a fourth and goal, Murray's lone option was to take off, and he did. He dove into the end zone, took a heck of a shot, and held onto the ball. The touchdown and extra point put Georgia up 38–37. The defense then did what it was supposed to do for three plays, forcing a fourth and 18 at the

Auburn 27-yard line. Auburn quarterback Nick Marshall launched a ball with Georgia defenders Tray Matthews and Josh Harvey-Clemons in coverage. But Harvey-Clemons knocked the ball away from Matthews, who was trying to intercept or bat it down. It bounced behind them and into Auburn receiver Ricardo Louis' hands for a 73-yard touchdown. Auburn would win 43–38, stunning Georgia after its magnificent comeback. After that game, however, Georgia won three in a row against Auburn. Perhaps the football gods have atoned with the recent wins for the manner in which the Bulldogs lost that one.

An interesting dynamic about the Georgia-Auburn rivalry is how so many important people associated with it have been on both sides and how intertwined it is. Legendary Georgia coach Vince Dooley played at Auburn and was an assistant before taking the Georgia job. Prior to the 1981 Sugar Bowl, in which Georgia was playing for the 1980 national championship, Auburn approached Dooley about a job. Dooley listened but turned it down. Pat Dye played under Wally Butts at Georgia but went on to be Auburn's coach from 1981 to 1992. Ralph "Shug" Jordan, who coached Auburn's football team from 1951 to 1975, was an assistant at Georgia from 1947 to 1950. Former Georgia athletic director Joel Eaves, who hired a little-known Dooley in 1964, coached Auburn's basketball team from 1949 to 1963.

As of early 2017, Georgia holds a 57–55–8 lead in the all-time series. Before the game was moved to each school's campus, the two teams met primarily in Columbus, Georgia, with the game being played there 37 times. The game has been played in Atlanta 15 times, Macon four times, Savannah two times, and Montgomery, Alabama, twice. The rivalry wasn't played at Auburn until 1960 and was held in Athens twice—in 1912 and 1929—before the series started rotating between campuses.

A lot of plays have been made in this storied rivalry that dates back to the early days of football in the South. It's a rivalry of historical significance that continues to add to the overall game's legacy today.

Other Sports Greats

Reminisce About the Greatest Bulldog Ever

O h, where to start.

Daniel Hamilton Magill Jr. was a jack of all trades around the University of Georgia athletics department. A bat boy, at first. Harry Mehre's assistant. Sports information director. Tennis coach. Historian. Magill did any and everything around the University of Georgia. A native of Athens, Magill was always around the university, which probably led to his love of the place.

Magill had a strong connection to the city from birth. On January 25, 1921, Magill became the first baby born at what is now Piedmont Athens Regional. He grew up in the city and became a bat boy for the Georgia baseball team when he was only 10. He'd attend college at Georgia, joining the Chi Phi fraternity and assisting Mehre when he was the football coach late into his tenure in Athens. In college Magill also lettered in both tennis and swimming, so he was quite the athlete too. In 1942 Magill graduated with a degree in journalism and later became the prep sports editor for *The Atlanta Journal* after World War II. Besides his time with *The Journal*, the only other time he spent away from Athens was when he was stationed around the country with the U.S. Marine Corps during the war.

He couldn't stay away from Athens. He loved to call himself an "All-American flunkie" since he stayed around the Classic City all the time. When Georgia football head coach and athletic director Wally Butts asked Magill to be his sports information director in 1949, Magill made the move back to Athens to work for his alma mater. A main part of the job was to promote the football team. Another part was to develop a following for the other sports at the university. And Magill went to work, personally covering every event as much as humanly possible for the university. These days sports information departments have a head for each sport with a graduate assistant or intern assisting them. Magill did just about everything himself. If he needed to be at a baseball game or a tennis match, he'd be there. More than anything, Magill loved to tell stories, especially those involving the history of the university and its athletics program.

One story Magill enjoyed telling was of Clegg Starks, a local boy whose first name was actually Pleas, but it was somehow misheard as Clegg, which stuck. Clegg was an African American boy who was always around the athletic fields because he was the son of the university chancellor's cook. Integration was a long ways away when Starks was around, and therefore he unfortunately never had a chance to showcase his athletic abilities on one of Georgia's football or baseball teams. But according to Magill, Starks could throw a football in the air 100 yards. Legend has it, according to Magill, that former head coach Herman Stegeman told some New York sportswriters about Starks' abilities with the football, and they didn't believe him. Stegeman collected bets, and Starks then launched a football down the field. When the ball traveled 100 yards, Starks and Stegeman split the winnings of the money lost by the New York sportswriters. Former Georgia quarterback Fran Tarkenton once told the *Athens Banner-Herald* that he saw Starks throw the ball 100 yards down the field and that the story is very much true. Starks was also a star pitcher, who Magill said once outdueled baseball Hall of Famer Satchel Paige in an All-Star game in Charleston, South Carolina.

If not for Magill repeating his story, the legend of Starks may have ceased to exist over time. But that's Magill in a nutshell. He loved to tell the tales that piqued the interest of his audience. And just about all of them had to do with the University of Georgia when he did talk. He saw a lot during the nearly 60 years he spent in an official work capacity with the athletics program. He also saw a lot as a child growing up in Athens.

Six years into his job as Georgia's sports information director, Georgia had an opening for a men's tennis coach. The Bulldogs were a floundering program at the time, and Butts told him to find a replacement. The problem was Magill couldn't find one. So he decided he'd do it in the short term until someone would emerge. Next thing you know, Magill went on to become arguably the greatest college tennis coach the sport has ever seen. In 34 years leading the Georgia tennis program, Magill compiled an astonishing 706–183 record with 13 SEC outdoor championships, eight SEC indoor championships, and two national championships. Georgia constructed a new tennis complex, which was named in his honor and today has 12 outdoor tennis courts and four indoor courts. With the NCAA going to the team format for its tennis championships, Magill partnered with the NCAA to let Georgia host the first 13 tournaments. The event has always generated a profit when in Athens, and a lot of the money goes back into upgrading the complex. In 2002 the complex underwent a $7.5 million renovation.

Magill turned Georgia's tennis program into one of the most elite in the history of the college sport. And there was still more on his plate outside of this and his sports information director duties. Two years before taking the tennis coaching job, Magill noticed that excitement over the football team was beginning to wane. Butts had some dominating teams in the 1940s, but the 1950s were off to a slow start. Magill hated that interest wasn't greater and decided to spring into action about fixing it. Magill founded the Georgia Bulldog Club to help fan support after noticing a despondent Butts one day complaining about how Georgia Tech was filling its stadium while Georgia struggled to get many fans to Athens.

So Magill went all over the state and set up Georgia Bulldog Clubs in all 159 counties, dubbing the organization, "The Majority Party of the Empire State of the South." It became a hit, and the UGA alumni came out to support the program through the bad times. Some may argue that Magill's genius in doing such a thing kept Georgia as the dominant football program in the state of Georgia for years to come.

Magill stayed on as sports information director until 1977. He retired as the men's tennis coach in 1988. He kept a role at UGA as the director of men's and women's tennis until retiring in 1995, though his retirement came after a dispute with the university on whether Title

Visit the ITA Men's Collegiate Tennis Hall of Fame

Nestled next to the Dan Magill Tennis Complex is a little treasure on campus. The ITA Men's Collegiate Tennis Hall of Fame stores a lot of history from the beginnings of college tennis, including 1,800 rare photos from its first class and many more in the groups since.

Former Georgia tennis coach Dan Magill used to give personal tours and would share stories about his experiences in college tennis. The Hall of Fame has been inducting classes since 1983. The most famous names inducted into the ITA Men's College Tennis Hall of Fame are Arthur Ashe (UCLA, 1983), Jimmy Connors (UCLA, 1986), John McEnroe (Stanford, 1996), and Patrick McEnroe (Stanford, 2008).

Georgia players inducted into the Hall of Fame are Mikael Pernfors (2000), Al Parker (2007), and Allen Miller (2007). Magill has been inducted as a coach. Also representing Georgia in the Hall of Fame as contributors are Col. John L. "Judge" Beaver and Gordon Smith.

IX applied to the women's tennis team and mandated equal access to the tennis stadium, which the university said it did. Although Magill was upset the university didn't side with him, he still kept his office at the ITA Men's Collegiate Tennis Hall of Fame, which is right next to the tennis complex named in his honor.

When reporters attend football games at Sanford Stadium, each person has a placard with their name and affiliation. Magill's was different. His read, "Dan Magill—Legend." And that's what he was at Georgia. A true legend with multiple encyclopedias of historical Georgia information in his brain. On Sunday, August 24, 2014, the greatest Bulldog ever died at the age of 93. Magill was magnificent for the program he adored so much. And the university is forever indebted to what Magill meant to it.

Take in a Tennis Match

Dan Magill only planned to coach the Georgia men's tennis team. Thirty-four years later, a great foundation was set. So who exactly would carry the torch? Replacing a legend is generally a tough thing for any program to do. But Manny Diaz was the perfect candidate to step in for Magill. He'd been familiar with how Magill ran such a successful program thanks to his playing days. As a late-blooming prospect from San Juan, Puerto Rico, Diaz, who became a member on four consecutive SEC championship teams, was recruited by Magill. After graduating, Diaz spent a year with Magill as a student assistant before returning to Puerto Rico to teach tennis at a resort.

Magill kept in touch and kept asking Diaz to return and be an assistant. By 1982 Diaz accepted and moved back to Athens. The pitch was that Magill would finish out his career and hand the tennis program over to Diaz. Before this could happen, Magill finally got over the hump with national championships in 1985 and 1987. After the 1988 season, Magill finally retired as Georgia's head coach and handed the reins over to Diaz.

Some coaches may find that kind of task tough. Diaz ran with it and built an even bigger power at Georgia over time. It took some time to recapture that national championship magic. Sure, Georgia dominated the SEC and advanced deep into every NCAA Tournament. Five times in Diaz's first 10 years, his teams finished as runners-up. His other five year-end finishes during this span were either in the quarterfinals or the semifinals.

In 1999 Georgia entered the NCAA Tournament as the No. 10 seed but got hot at the right time. The Bulldogs advanced to the national championship and faced UCLA, and the tournament took place at the Dan Magill Tennis Complex. Georgia won the doubles point but then dropped two matches to fall behind 2–1. UCLA was then able to take a 3–2 lead and came within a tiebreaker of winning. Instead, Georgia's

Isner's Time at Georgia

John Isner surprised himself with how his professional career has gone. Even he couldn't have guessed he'd go on to be one of the better American tennis players in a decade's worth of time. But in 2012 Isner reached as high as No. 9 in the world and enjoyed a great deal of success on the ATP Tour thanks to his nearly unreturnable serve. He'd go down in tennis lore thanks to a three-day tennis match at Wimbledon in 2010 against Nicolas Mahut that lasted 11 hours and five minutes.

But before Isner became the marathon man of the tennis ranks, he was a star college player at Georgia. In his first year, Isner was named the SEC's Freshman of the Year and was selected to the All-SEC first team. He also reached the NCAA doubles final with teammate Bo Hodge. A year later in 2005, Isner teamed up with Antonio Ruiz to win the doubles championship. Isner followed that up with an ITA All-American national championship win during the fall season against Baylor's Lars Poerschke. It was around this time that it became apparent Isner was more than just a college talent.

Since his college days, no one has really been able to touch his serve. Isner, who stands at 6'10", has been known to frequently fire his first serves in the mid-140 mph range. The fastest serve he's ever recorded clocked in at 157.2 mph, which is the fastest ever at an ATP or Davis Cup event. It's also the third fastest serve of all time. Professional tennis players have a hard enough time handling Isner's serves. Can you imagine what it was like for college players during his day?

Isner had a great junior year in 2006 but came back for his senior season in 2007 to deliver a national championship for his team. Isner became the No. 1 player for the majority of the singles season and checked in at No. 1 as well at doubles with partner Luis Flores. While he would not win a singles or doubles championship as a senior, Isner led a talented Georgia team to an undefeated season and a national championship. And that's what coming back for one final year was all about.

Michael Lang held off UCLA's Marcin Rozpedski and forced a third set on court six. Lang would win along with Joey Pitts on court four, giving the Bulldogs Diaz's first national championship.

From there, Diaz kept the machine rolling. Georgia won the national championship again in 2001 with a 4–1 victory against Tennessee. Georgia's 2007 team defeated Illinois in the national title match 4–0, becoming only the seventh college tennis team to record a sweep in the finals. This team featured John Isner, who would go on to be one of the better American professional tennis players during the 2010s. In 2008 Georgia caught fire late in the year and advanced to the national championship again. The Bulldogs defeated Texas 4–2 for Diaz's fourth national title. In total Diaz has six national championships as he also led Georgia to two ITA National Indoor titles in 2006 and 2007. Before the 2017 season, Diaz held a 651–140 career record as a head coach, which is good for a .823 winning percentage.

Diaz isn't the only head tennis coach at Georgia who has accomplished big things. Women's head coach Jeff Wallace took over his program in 1985 just a season after his last as a player under Magill. Wallace quickly turned Georgia's fortunes around and got the Bulldogs to the national championship in 1987. The Bulldogs lost to Stanford, but a foundation was set for the program to begin flourishing.

Georgia hosted the women's national championship for the first time ever in 1994, which certainly benefited the Bulldogs. This team was one of the best in the history of the sport, considering it posted an overall record of 27–2 and went 14–0 in SEC play. The Bulldogs won the SEC Tournament and won the USTA/ITA National Team Indoor Championship. All that was left was the NCAA Tournament. And, of course, Georgia was able to get it done. Wallace recorded his first national championship with a 5–4 win against Stanford, and his team celebrated on its home court.

Six years later in 2000, Wallace and the Bulldogs got back to that particular moment. Georgia faced the familiar foe in Stanford, but this time the championship match was on Pepperdine's campus. And once

John Isner, the 6'10" tennis player who would go on to become a professional star, and Antonio Ruiz celebrate after winning the NCAA doubles national championship in 2005. (AP Images)

again it came down to the final match. Georgia was able to win again and recorded a 5–4 victory and an NCAA title.

Since Wallace became the Georgia women's tennis team's head coach, he's recorded two national titles and three USTA/ITA Indoor Team National Championships. Prior to the 2017 season, Wallace totaled 677 career wins, 14 SEC titles, and was named ITA National Coach of the Year four times.

Celebrate Yoculan's Dominance

No team performed at gymnastics the way Georgia did for 26 years under Suzanne Yoculan. She was a mastermind coach and quite possibly the best recruiter the sport has ever seen. Soon after her arrival to Georgia, Yoculan began stockpiling talent and winning meets. In her first year, Yoculan placed Georgia ninth overall at the NCAA championships. That's good and all, but it was only the beginning of a dynasty that would last for two and a half decades.

Yoculan's first national championship came in 1987 during her fourth season as Georgia's head coach. In Salt Lake City, Georgia was able to score a championship-winning 187.900, which bested the Utah Red Rocks' score of 187.550. From there the Gym Dogs would win national titles in 1989, 1993, 1998, and 1999. The 1993, 1998, and 1999 titles all saw undefeated seasons from Georgia. From 1984 to 2001, Georgia scored 26 individual titles as well.

After a few seasons without a national title, Georgia kicked it up a notch, beginning in 2005, though it almost didn't happen. A poor meet in the Southeast Regional saw Georgia make the NCAA Championships as the 12th seed—the last in the event. If the Gym Dogs were left out of the 2005 championships, it would have been the first time since 1983 for that to occur. But Georgia got in and made the most of it. It went from being the last team in to winning the whole thing, surprising just about everyone else at the championships.

"We knew the stars had to align for Georgia to win," Yoculan said. "This championship isn't just for this group of girls here tonight. This one is for every girl that has been on our teams since the championship team in 1999. We spent a lot of time working together to get back to where we were before the regionals. I knew the regional was just a fluke. Lightning doesn't strike Georgia twice in a row. We emphasized the total team aspect. Everyone on this team had a role in what happened. We had to tighten the screws up. The girls responded well. They did everything we asked of them."

That 2005 title set off a run like no other. From that title through the 2009 season, the Gym Dogs won five national championships in a row. This marked the first time a team did this since Utah did so from 1982 to 1986.

Yoculan's 2006 team featured five first-team All-Americans led by Courtney Kupets, who earned her recognition for the all-around, uneven bars, balance beam, and floor exercise. This Gym Dogs team went 36–0, won a 15th SEC title, and dominated everyone it faced.

Kupets' addition marked a new era for the Gym Dogs, considering Kupets had just competed for the United States at the 2004 Olympics in Athens, Greece. But Tiffany Tolnay, Katie Heenan, Nikki Childs, and Kelsey Ericksen all did their part to crush their opponents. All four of these gymnasts ended the season with first-team All-American status, showcasing the pure dominance of this team. "This team was very special," Yoculan said. "We set a goal at the beginning of the season to be undefeated. We wanted to strive for perfection, and that perfection was going to be an undefeated season. I'm just so proud of them to not only hand Georgia its seventh national championship, but also a fourth undefeated season. And that just really is a testament of their dedication and their work ethic and their focusing the entire season from the Cancun meet to the end."

The 2007 team dealt with injuries to Ericksen and Ashley Kupets late in the season and were forced to make some lineup changes. Even so, that didn't stop the Gym Dogs from recording a third consecutive national championship. Courtney Kupets became the first gymnast to win back-to-back all-around titles that year since Georgia's Kim Arnold in 1997–98.

Georgia then recorded a fourth consecutive national championship in 2008 with 197.450 points, and Utah coming in second with 197.125. By this point it had become commonplace for Yoculan's Gym Dogs to win national championships.

So it didn't surprise anyone when Georgia won another national championship in 2009, marking the fifth in a row for the program. Led by Courtney Kupets' career-best 39.9 all-around score, Georgia was able to send Yoculan into retirement with her 10th career national title. It also placed Georgia atop the national title leaders in gymnastics, besting Utah's previous best of nine. "We all wanted to send Suzanne back with something to remember," gymnast Grace Taylor said. "It was an amazing championship. It couldn't get better than this. It was beautiful, and we're so honored that we got to be part of this last year for her."

Check Out Championship-Laden Diamond Dogs

In 1990 Georgia's baseball team was thought to be a team that would give teams fits or possibly compete for an SEC title. And for much of the season, the Diamond Dogs led by head coach Steve Webber consistently put away opponents.

But at the worst possible time, the Diamond Dogs began a cold spell and dropped five games in a row to close the season, including two in the SEC Tournament. There was a real worry that the late losing streak might have cost Georgia a spot in the NCAA Tournament. But when it came time to select teams, Georgia was offered a No. 2 seed in the Northeast Regional. Handed an opportunity to forget what tribulations they'd just been through, the Diamond Dogs took it upon themselves to start over and create a new story about how this particular season would end.

In the opening round, Georgia drew No. 5-seeded Connecticut, and the Diamond Dogs took care of business 7–2. Georgia then defeated No. 4-seeded Maine 6–3 and top-seeded North Carolina 5–4 in consecutive games to reach the regional championship. There, the Bulldogs got Rutgers and dropped the first game 4–3. In the deciding game, however, the Diamond Dogs got their revenge and drubbed the Scarlet Knights 20–9. The win moved Georgia to the College World Series in Omaha, Nebraska, where it was re-seeded fourth overall out of eight.

The Diamond Dogs drew Mississippi State in the first round and moved on with a 3–0 win. In the second round, Georgia dispatched Stanford 16–2, and the Cardinal were forced to face Mississippi State in an elimination game. Stanford won and got to face Georgia again in the semifinals. This time, the Cardinal picked up a 4–2 win, setting up an elimination game rubber match. This meant Georgia's Mike Rebhan had to face Stanford's Mike Mussina for the second time in the College World Series. Rebhan pitched a brilliant game, holding the Cardinal to only six hits. Meanwhile, Georgia was able to get the bats rolling en route to a 5–1 win. The victory advanced Georgia to the finals to take on Oklahoma State.

Seeded third in its bracket, the Cowboys dismantled their opponents in three games without a loss. But it was winner take all in this College World Series final. Even though Oklahoma State scored 35 runs in its three past games, Webber decided to tab freshman left-hander Stan Payne as his starter for the game. Payne came through for Webber, keeping the Cowboys scoreless for five innings until giving up a run in the sixth. Georgia had previously scored two runs and held a 2–1 lead when Webber changed pitchers from Payne to Dave Fleming in the seventh inning. Never mind the fact that Oklahoma State's offense was hot in Omaha. On this particular day, the Cowboys' bats could not handle the Georgia pitchers consistently. Following Payne's lead, Fleming retired eight of 10 batters, which included striking out the side in the ninth inning. Georgia defeated Oklahoma State 2–1 and won its first ever national championship at the College World Series. Georgia may have closed its regular season on a sour note. But it sure finished its year on the highest mountain possible. "We were just fortunate today to have two good pitchers who could stop their hitting," Webber said after the game. "That's what this game boiled down to."

In total the Diamond Dogs have appeared six times in the College World Series. The first was in 1987, and others came in 1990, 2001, 2004, and 2006. But it wasn't until 2008 that Georgia and head coach David Perno were able to get a taste of what was experienced in 1990 with a national championship.

Going into the year, many expected the Diamond Dogs to be a pretty good team but not necessarily a national title-contending team. But there were certainly some great players returning to this team, including shortstop Gordan Beckham, pitcher Justin Grimm, pitcher Joshua Fields, and outfielder Matt Cerione. They played an incredibly tough schedule and finished the regular season and SEC Tournament 35–21–1, which led to a No. 1 seed in the Athens Regional. The first game did not go as planned as No. 4 seed Lipscomb upset the Bulldogs 10–7. Sent to the losers bracket, the Diamond Dogs had to beat Louisville 9–8 before getting even with Lipscomb 14–3 in a rematch. This set up a best-of-three regional championship series with Georgia Tech. The Diamond Dogs blew out the Yellow Jackets in two games, winning 8–0 and 18–6 to advance to the super regional. Facing N.C. State, Georgia was taken to three games, but the Diamond Dogs won 17–8 in the final game. This got the Bulldogs into the College World Series as a No. 8 seed.

Georgia upset No. 1 seed Miami in the first round 7–4 and then defeated Stanford 4–3 in Omaha. Sitting at 2–0 in the winners bracket, the Diamond Dogs waited on the rest to take care of itself, which eventually ended up being Stanford eliminating Miami. A rematch with the Cardinal was on hand, and the Diamond Dogs won 10–8. For the first time since 1990, Georgia was back in the championship series.

This was a wacky College World Series with quite the upsets. Joining Georgia in the championship series was Fresno State, a team seeded fourth in its regional. But as can happen in baseball, Fresno State caught fire. The Diamond Dogs took the first game of the series 7–6, and Beckham hit his 27th home run during the game. But Fresno State came back and took the second game in a 19–10 shootout. That set up a final game between the two schools for it all. Fresno State pitcher Justin Wilson put in a brilliant performance as the Bulldogs held the Diamond Dogs scoreless for seven innings. Meanwhile, Fresno State outfielder Steve Detwiler hit two homers and accounted for five runs. Georgia came as close as possible to a second national championship. Instead, Fresno State capped one of the most miraculous title runs in NCAA baseball history.

Bring Out Bauerle's Best

Jack Bauerle is the type to remember losses more than wins. Well, the good thing is that, at least with the Georgia women's swimming and diving team, there haven't been too many losses since he took over head coaching duties in 1979. But it would take some time for Bauerle to record his first national championship. That didn't come until 1999, but the wait was well worth it, as any championship at that level would be.

From there, however, Georgia would be in the mix just about every year when it came to the women's national championships. Under Bauerle, the Lady Bulldogs have won seven national championships. In addition to the 1999 title, Georgia's women have won titles in 2000, 2001, 2005, 2013, 2014, and 2016. The women also finished as runners-up in 2002, 2003, 2004, 2006, 2009, 2011, 2012, and 2015.

Bauerle's been able to build a winner with the women's program, which has featured 163 All-Americans, including Olympic swimmer Allison Schmitt. Georgia's women have finished in the top 10 an amazing 28 times since 1979 and have won 12 SEC championships. Bauerle has also been recognized as the National Women's Swimming and Diving Coach of the Year seven times and earned the same honor from the SEC 16 times.

With the women his career record prior to the 2017–18 season was 318–34–2. One of the more impressive streaks through all of these accomplishments was being able to win 100 consecutive meets at the Gabrielsen Natatorium, which began in 1995. On January 30, 2016, the Lady Bulldogs defeated Wisconsin in a dual meet and recorded win No. 100 in a row at home.

"It's a funny feeling. You feel like you've seen a moment flash in front of your eyes," Bauerle said. "It's a great feeling, a little bit of relief. It's also a feeling of appreciation more than anything else. Certainly it makes you feel pride for our program."

Bauerle took over the men's swimming and diving program in 1983 and has been named the SEC Coach of the Year twice (1992, 1997) and has helped develop 20 individual NCAA championship winners. The Georgia men have finished in the top 10 an impressive 16 times under Bauerle, and Bauerle recorded a 221–91–1 all-time record prior to the 2016–17 season.

One of the biggest honors Bauerle ever received was being able to serve as the head coach for the U.S. Women's Olympic Team during the 2008 Olympics in Beijing. Bauerle was also an assistant coach for the U.S. Men's Olympic Team during the 2016 Olympics in Rio de Janeiro. "Any time I get to represent the USA and UGA at the Olympics, it's a real honor," Bauerle said when he was selected for the Rio Games. "I am absolutely elated to be chosen. I'm very thankful and I'm excited. It will be a busy time for all of us, but we're going to make a lot of special memories."

Acknowledgments

From the earliest memories of social interaction, I was surrounded by Georgia football. Born at Northside Hospital in Atlanta, my parents had already moved to the tiny town of Madison, Georgia. About six years later, our family moved to Oconee County—not quite Athens but not exactly Watkinsville. We had an Athens address, but we were right on the border of Oconee County and Clarke County. We considered ourselves Athenians, though Athenians would beg to differ.

Regardless, where I lived throughout my life—except for a four-year span in my late 20s —has been in Bulldog country. Therefore, writing a book like this didn't require reaching out to people I'd never spoken to before or heading to an unfamiliar library to research.

Day-to-day conversations with fellow reporters, local Georgia football aficionados, those within the Georgia athletics department, and friends who follow the Bulldogs were easy to have. It's a football-crazed city that hosts the most important football team in the state. Sure, the NFL has a team in Atlanta. But college football is king in most southern states. That certainly applies to a state like Georgia.

Whether it's for a project like this or for my full-time job as a Georgia beat reporter, the sports information crew led by Claude Felton probably rarely receives the respect or recognition it deserves. Felton's team has long been accommodating in just about any way. His group is a helpful bunch, including Mike Mobley, Leland Barrow, Steven Colquitt, Christopher Lakos, Brandon Weiss, Whitney Tarpy, and Karen Huff. Without them, this job would be a lot harder than it is.

About those four years away from Georgia: in early 2011 my then-girlfriend received a job opportunity in Washington, D.C., so I inquired about one in a nearby area with CBSSports.com, the company I was working with at the time. I ended up moving to Maryland and spent three total years covering the Baltimore Ravens, among other areas of coverage. By the end I was a blogger for CBSSports.com and covering preps for *The Washington Post*.

Then an opportunity to return home occurred. I was offered and accepted a job to cover UGA for *The Telegraph* in Macon, Georgia. If not for Daniel Shirley and Sherrie Marshall, I wouldn't be in Athens and I wouldn't have been able to write this book. I must thank them for giving me the opportunity to return home to cover this program.

Most importantly, however, I must thank my wife, Lauren—the aforementioned girlfriend I chased up to the D.C. area. I moved away from home for her; she moved back home for me. Without Lauren, nothing I've accomplished to date would have been possible.

Sources

Columbia Daily Spectator

The Exponent Telegram

The State

Pro Football Hall of Fame

ESPN's *SEC Storied: Miracle 3*

ESPN's *SEC Storied: Herschel*

Loran Smith, ed., *Between the Hedges: 100 Years of Georgia Football*

Cale Conley, *War Between the States*

Patrick Garbin, *About Them Dawgs!: Georgia Football's Memorable Teams and Players*

Patrick Garbin, *I Love Georgia/I Hate Florida*

John Stegeman, *The Ghosts of Herty Field*

Bill Cromartie, *Clean Old-fashioned Hate: Georgia Vs. Georgia Tech.*

Vince Dooley with Blake Giles, *Vince Dooley's Tales From the 1980 Season*

"The Man Who Broke The Drought," *Georgia Trend Magazine,* Gene Asher

"A Debatable Football Scandal in the Southeast," *Sports Illustrated*, Dan Jenkins.

"Mark Richt and Wally Butts could have carried on quite the conversation about the forward pass," *Athens Banner-Herald*, Loran Smith.

"Georgia strong-armed OSU to win title," *Omaha World-Herald*, Steve Pivovar

"Smith: Stanfill recalls classic moments," *Athens Banner-Herald*, Loran Smith

"Officials: timeout call was the right one in last Saturday's Florida-Georgia game," AP

"They're Not All Kicking and Screaming Over the Absence of Tee," *Los Angeles Times*, Jim Litke

"Title enabled Dooley to retire happy man," *Athens Banner-Herald*, Josh Kendall